GOLDEN AGE, GOLDEN EARTH
ANNI SENNOV

good adventures publishing

GOLDEN AGE, GOLDEN EARTH

©2015, Anni Sennov and Good Adventures Publishing
First edition, second impression
Set with Cambria
Layout: Anni Sennov – www.sennovpartners.com
Cover design: Michael Bernth – www.monovoce.dk
Cover and Author photo: Semko Belcerski - www.semko.dk

Original title in Danish:
"Den Gyldne Jord"
Translated into English by: Lotte and David Young
Proofread and adapted by: Sue Jonas Dupuis

ISBN 978-87-92549-74-7

CONTENTS

NOTICE

The purpose of this book is to inform you about planet Earth and some of the influences coming from 'outer space' (other places). Out and about in the Cosmos, political correctness is not quite as it is on Earth. Therefore, I ask you to read this book in a spirit of open-mindedness. It is absolutely not my intention to offend any specific groups or people here on Earth but rather to show things from various different angles.

A sense of humour is usually a great tool to have when mingling with the various energies that come to planet Earth and I have had many good laughs while writing this book.

Everything I have written is based on what I see and sense energetically and clairvoyantly, therefore we cannot know for sure if things truly are as I see and sense them.

Although the author (Anni Sennov) and the publisher have made every effort to ensure the accuracy and completeness of information contained in this book, we assume no responsibility for errors, inaccuracies, omissions, or any inconsistency herein. Any offence caused to people, places, or organisations is unintentional.

Readers should use their own judgment or consult a holistic medical expert or their personal physician for specific applications to their individual problems.

Anni Sennov

FOREWORD

Planet Earth is a project, a place where we come to experiment, learn and play in the myriad possibilities that constitute our human lives. Anything and everything is possible here - the good, the bad and everything in between. If you have ever asked yourself what you are doing on planet Earth, it is because somehow you may feel that there are greater mysteries that, as yet, remain unfathomed. Maybe you feel that you do not quite belong here or else that you really *do* belong here and yet nobody seems to notice you. Maybe you would like to know exactly what to do to be happier and more fulfilled here on Earth, or you would like to understand the various 'invisible' influences at work to better understand your fellow humans. Above all, you would like to know where we are headed...

In this, her 22nd book, Anni Sennov, pioneer in the field of consciousness, shows us that we have every reason to be excited and optimistic about what lies ahead. She shares her unique insight into the planetary origins of some of the quirks of humanity with her usual trademark frankness. She also explains the technical aspects of the New Time energy structures and their ramifications. She has been at the forefront of energy technology since she founded AuraTransformation™ over 15 years ago and has dedicated her life to helping others live more joyfully. Believe me, Anni walks her talk. Rest assured, the future is Golden!

Life is such a wonderful adventure and if you want to jump in with both (Golden) feet, this book will show you how. Be your truth and you will get all the help you need!

With much love and optimism,

Sue Jonas Dupuis

INTRODUCTION

Earth is home to a dualistic energy and all the inherent contradictions of this duality are present on this planet. Everything here is divided into spirit and matter, light and dark, good and evil, and so on.

At least that is how it was until now, as spirit energy is beginning to take form and become visible for all to see, feel and sense and even hear, smell and taste. This is going to be very significant for the future development of planet Earth.

This is also the ultimate purpose of this book; to explain the fusion between the spiritual and the condensed material energies. This fusion means that the spirit helps raise the frequency of the material energy making it purer, yet still visible. The material energy therefore becomes visible at a much higher frequency level of consciousness that it would not otherwise be able to reach by itself.

This means that it is now possible for us humans to succeed to a much greater extent than we have ever been able to before, as long as we have positive intentions and think holistically in everything we undertake. It is important that we do not do things exclusively for our own gain but that each of us tries to contribute the best we can to raise the levels of balance, consciousness and knowledge all over Planet Earth.

Earth is a pure and holy planet with a unique development potential. It is a place where everything good can succeed for those who are ready to live a life of love, balance and harmony both within and without.

Earth is a Whole but it has an infinite number of aspects within itself, each with its unique expression. Whether it is in the form of human beings, animals, plants, crystals, microbes, etc., it is not enough to think only about your nearest and dearest, about your own children and grandchildren and their balance and their future if you want to do something beneficial. You also need to think about the bigger picture and about our planet!

I therefore invite you to read my book about the Golden Earth, the Golden creation and the creative force, which, in cooperation with the love-intelligent Crystal energy, leads us to fresh insights and totally new heights and glorious of positivity on the human and spiritual-material level here on Earth.

With love,

Anni Sennov

CREATION AND THE CREATIVE FORCE

Earth is not just the home of dualistic energy. It is also the home of Creation, the Creative Force and of the feminine and masculine aspects.

Both spirit and matter exist here, where matter is spirit in a condensed form. If spirit does not have matter as a counterforce, it is impossible for it to create visible and measurable energy that we humans can relate to on the physical level. This means that if creation and the creative force do not cooperate in every aspect of the materialisation, realisation and visualisation of things and situations on this Earth, it will be impossible to make anything materialise. Imagine having an idea that you talk a lot about but never actually do anything to make it happen. It hangs in the air like a spiritual impulse that intuitive people with a sense for non-material energies can feel but it is never realised or manifested on the physical level.

Physical and material creation can thus only happen if there is a spiritual impulse and a creative force present which serve as the catalyst for creation and the continuing creative process.

Generally speaking, we can equate the creative force with masculine energy and creation itself with feminine energy, where the creative force and creation (the creation force) contain both masculine and feminine energy. There is nothing on Planet Earth that is exclusively masculine or feminine. Everything terrestrial contains duality.

Earth is one of the very few places in the entire Cosmos where all creation takes place on a very physical and visible level, even if the spirit is fully present in the creative act. This is seen most clearly in the creation of physical life. The presence of two opposing physical energies in the form of an egg and a sperm cell is necessary here, each one having a spiritual and materialising or manifesting impulse in itself, thus enabling creation.

The continued creation process of pregnancy also consists of two essential, opposing, spiritual-material energies. It is here that the desire to create life exists, along with the fear of losing life (the child), which is why spirit and matter can sometimes have problems cooperating in the design of the new individual.

Birth also consists of two opposing energies, a spiritual releasing energy which causes the mother's system to release the child into freedom and welcome it into the physical world as well as a physical energy which creates the physical pain in her body which causes the expulsion of the child from the womb, thereby making the child's energy detach from that of the mother's.

Regarding all creation on Earth, we can therefore see that it consists of two seemingly incompatible energies - a spiritual, creative, initiating impulse combined with a material energy consisting of hard work on the physical, mental and/or emotional level in order to realise new projects, ideas and physical life.

GOOD AND EVIL
- EARTH'S SPIRITUAL CREATIONS

Earth can be Heaven for those who think and create positively but it can be Hell for those who are ruled by conflict, fear and negative energies, or who surround themselves with negative creation.

It is unlikely that anyone who is in the midst of war and chaos would ever agree that we all help to create the framework of our own lives whilst those who manage to escape may well simply imagine that good fortune has smiled upon them.

However, if you use your spiritual impulse and listen to your intuition, it is possible to pick up on external energies, as well as information about future events. It really is possible to get away in time and find yourself safe as disaster strikes elsewhere, because you chose to listen to your inner voice, even though there may have been no physical evidence that the things you were sensing would happen in the future. If therefore you get a feeling that something specific is going to happen, even though it may seem totally illogical, make the decision to be your own best friend and listen to yourself.

The very best and the very worst that you can possibly imagine co-exist on this Earth. There are also many things that you could never possibly imagine, even in your wildest dreams, because you are made of different stuff from those who created such things or situations.

Admirable goodness and detestable evil exist here, along with light and dark energies, both of which can express themselves in a good or evil, a positive or a negative, way. There is nothing written in stone regarding how people ought to think, feel and behave here on Earth. We can see this clearly in the widely differing laws and religions that exist in various countries the world over. There is not just one way to live which is better than another, even though many people may think that they have found the definitive truth about life.

Earth consists of many different entities and individuals who come here from virtually the whole of the Cosmos. So, if you can imagine the Cosmos as being one enormous human body, people, monsters and many other entities come to Earth from the cosmic heart, brain, liver, kidneys, buttocks... respectively. There are even individuals and entities from the feet and the toes of the Cosmos, as well as from the respiratory tract. Earth is in fact a spiritual-material development planet which acts as a global information centre for the creation energy of all existing universes in the entire Cosmos.

As we know, Earth is the home of creation and the creative force, so anything can be done here if there is the insight, imagination and ability to carry it out. The entire cosmic creation has its home here, deep within Planet Earth and it is here that the most interesting, crazy and violent projects are tested, projects which cannot be tested on a material level out in the Cosmos, because there are few places out there where material energy actually exists.

We are living right on top of the home of the divine creation and creative force, which, of course, has a knock-on effect on the possibilities that we humans have at our disposal to make a success of our lives on every level. This is the real reason why Earth has always been an extremely popular destination for entities and individuals from other universes who have wanted to come here in large numbers to be born as human beings. Here, they have the opportunity to develop in extraordinary ways, as well as to test their personal and cosmic consciousnesses and insight more rapidly and more intensely than is possible in many other places in the Cosmos.

Today, it is possible to develop your personal and cosmic consciousness at a highly accelerated rate, as Earth is about to undergo an extraordinary rise in frequency.

With the end of the Mayan calendar and the beginning of Earth's own chronology with a focus on creative leadership, which according to most sources took place on 21 December 2012, Earth actually went from belonging to the liver-universe to belonging to the creative universe in the cosmic uterus and prostate. In overall terms, this means that the entire population of Earth now has the possibility of creating whatever it desires, as soon as people have learned what to choose and what to reject in their own lives.

If they do not choose for the benefit of both themselves and the Whole, they will remain in the liver-universe. Here the main focus is on learning to differentiate between usable and non-usable energies while Earth continues its development in the creative universe along with the people who are able to make the right choices for the benefit of themselves and the Whole.

This optimal opportunity to become an independent creative individual will, in the future, cause even more external entities and individuals than usual to make their way towards Earth. That means that we will see an extraordinary increase in population in new areas of the Earth in the coming years, without there being any logical explanation for this other than regular growth in those areas.

Many will still come here even though they will not actually like being here. The reason being that the opportunity to develop in an optimal way, by living and expressing themselves on the physical level through a creative spiritual-material body, is clearly greater than the discomfort and challenge of being trapped in a human body.

Being able to have the opportunity to create their own masterpieces for better or for worse in the versatile universe that Planet Earth represents is undeniably very attractive to most of them.

ALL LIFE STARTS WITH FREE WILL

Free will is the magical concept for creation here on Earth, be it for destiny or for success.

At the dawn of time, the concept of free will was – and still is – the first impulse with which we, as human beings, were equipped in our personal consciousnesses, before we were even born. Free will precedes everything, even the feeling of love, bodily desires, karma/destiny and dharma/life purpose, because each and every one of us decides whether to be born or not.

If as yet unborn children change their minds at the last minute before being born, they always have the possibility of opting out, even though they had originally agreed to be born. They also have the right to die and leave the physical plane whenever they want; no one is here against their will. However, it may well be that they change their minds while they are here because they did not really understand what they were getting themselves into before they came here. No spiritual beings can imagine what it is like to live and express themselves through a physical body, unless they have previously incarnated on Earth.

Everyone has the possibility of living life as they choose, even though they are subject to karma, a certain life destiny and path of development. This is because as soon as they become aware of why certain things happen in their lives, they can choose to change both their direction and also their physical environment. In return, they must live with the consequences of their choices if those around them choose not to move forward or develop with them. Unfortunately people often do not have adequate protection and resilience on a personal level to remain in balance during the adjustment phase. This is why many people choose to stay exactly where they are.

Everyone also has the freedom of choice to be 'good' or 'evil' and every person has the freedom to reject evil and misery in their lives. There is just no certainty that it can be done in the company of the specific individuals with whom they have chosen to live their lives. So the concept of free will can embody many more aspects than just learning to say "yes" and "no" to certain things.

Just because you become more aware and evolved as a person, it doesn't mean that you will automatically be allowed to raise the energy of other people and bring them out of misery, simply because you love them and want to help them. Each individual needs to have their own desire to evolve and each individual has to take the required path for this on the human and consciousness levels. No one else can do it for anyone else when it comes to integrating the non-material and spiritual values of life. However, it is still always possible to pay to get physical (non-spiritual) things done by others.

NOTHING STAYS THE SAME

Each period of development here on Earth has a specific over-all guiding frequency and vibration of its own. This frequency includes myriad underlying frequencies and guidelines which indicate the direction in which Earth's development and creation is expected to go over the given time period.

As the creation energy here on Earth is in perpetual motion towards the new, it is never possible to return to a previous state where everything remains as it once was. This is because either you have changed physically, personally and consciously, or your environment has. This means that nothing can ever stay the same and for that reason alone, we can say that something has evolved. It can be up or down, depending solely on the observer's point of view. For example, one party to a divorce can experience it as setback, while the other may see it as a step forward.

Purely on the level of consciousness, Earth is positioned on a so-called 'development belt' in the Cosmos where the planet is part of a larger collaboration with the other planets of our solar system, as well as with selected planets in other solar systems and galaxies.

Depending on where the overall guiding frequency lies on the 'development belt', information is continually being released in the form of creative and instinctive impulses from Earth's inner consciousness layer to all living things on Earth's surface. These impulses correspond to the human and technological developments which are expected to take place in that given time period.

Earth's overall development is thereby stimulated thanks to instinctive impulses emitted from some deeper-lying and more heavily vibrating energy layers in the Earth's interior. These impulses are most often of a more condensed and physically perceptible non-spiritual nature and they represent only a very small, yet powerful, part of Earth's total consciousness. The scale of these impulses in relation to our consciousness can be likened to how little space the reptilian brain takes up in the human body in relation to the disproportionate effect it has on human behaviour.

The energy in the instinctive and basic impulses which is released from Earth's deep layers of consciousness to motivate all new development on the planet can best be captured by people – rich and poor, good and evil – who have an instinctive and survival-oriented creative impulse in them; in other words, by more instinctive people who are able to see possibilities in everything that is substantially condensed and material in its structure, as well as by people who are very body and money-focused in their approach to life.

The energy can also be detected by very spiritual people who are not particularly focused on the material aspect of existence. Hyper-sensitive and very spiritual people can sense the instinctive impulses coming from Earth's interior in a completely different way from the aforementioned instinctive types.

Many spiritual people perceive and sense events and changes on the invisible level instead of seeing and feeling them physically. So instead of constantly looking, like a latter-day Sherlock Holmes, for physical evidence which can prove that certain things really have happened, spiritual people register that those changes have taken place by being in contact with the invisible, unconscious, subconscious or superconscious energy on both the emotional and the mental levels either in a place or around a person. This means that they notice these changes in what many perceive as a physical vacuum; in the air, in the atmosphere, in the energy, in a space or in the aura and radiance around a particular person. Here they can clearly sense if any recent changes have taken place and they can often equally clearly spot what those changes are.

The instinctive and basic impulses can therefore be detected both by very materially focused people and by those who are very spiritually focused. This enables Earth to maintain its overall spiritual-material balance without becoming too material and condensed in its structure.

The more spiritually aware people there are being born on Planet Earth, the more spiritually focused the planet will be able to become without losing its material and physically visible energy structure. Spirit is in fact integrated progressively deeper into matter with each new era on Earth, so both spirit and matter increase their overall consciousnesses, which we could describe as integration at the highest level.

SHARING EXPERIENCES IS IMPORTANT FOR EARTH'S CONTINUED DEVELOPMENT

Many young people and others who focus on the New Time will probably think that historians who write about everything that happens in the world are irrelevant. Development is happening so rapidly that it makes no sense to dwell on the events of yesterday and the more distant past. However, world history is not only recorded so that people can read about the past. World history is also written to make it easier for people, now and in the future, to follow human development during a given era and also to understand that development.

If we do not record our physical history and knowledge and thereby share everything that has so far been experienced in a terrestrial context, future generations will never have the possibility of learning from the successes and failures of previous generations. They would never be able to make choices in the light of other methods or solutions that have already been tested by past generations. They would always have to start from scratch when trying to solve any problem creatively. It is therefore extremely important for Earth's development on all levels that we share our experiences, otherwise we risk losing a lot of knowledge, insight and experience.

If we humans did not share our respective experiences and knowledge with others, many of us would have to face the exact same challenges in life, which would be pointless, as development would then stagnate and human ignorance would cause Earth to decline because of pollution, unhealthy lifestyles, war, etc. Without the knowledge of previous generations and their experiences it would be difficult to have an understanding of the bigger picture and therefore to know how to do things differently each time around. It would be impossible to focus on the integration of diverse energies from other people, cultures and communities, as well as from different places in and outside the solar system, which is currently the main purpose of all life on Earth. Moreover, it would be difficult to raise people's consciousnesses from the survival and reproduction phase to the integration and development phase.

The same basic life story would be repeated endlessly throughout the generations and Planet Earth's creative energy would stall. Creative energy cannot be reconciled with frequent repetition or by routine, unless the underlying consciousness is constantly changing direction. Ignorance, oppression, injustice, abuse of power, disease, war and many other negatively charged terrestrial conditions would constitute daily life everywhere on Earth because there would simply be no scope for development.

These days, all kinds of textbooks, medical books, self-development guides as well scholarly books and databases give us a wealth of recent history and the latest updates within each field. Due to Earth's combination of spiritual-material energy, these sorts of updating and upgrading are much more important here than anywhere else in the Cosmos. Here on Earth, many things get forgotten and remain on the invisible spiritual level in human thoughts, feelings and minds if they are not brought about, carried out and disseminated on the physical-material level. The physical-material level is the only place where everything is truly visible to everyone, which is why we perceive it as being our everyday 'conscious level', where we need to be physically awake and alert to keep pace and to cope.

What is happening in people's thoughts, emotions and minds is not always visible to all and is often associated with the unconscious, subconscious or superconscious level, depending on each individual. By creating and living new experiences as well as by writing, speaking and reading about them, we are actually helping to create history and share experiences for the benefit of all.

By writing this book, I am hoping to make a positive contribution to the world with my insight into the Earth's energy structure, function and role in developing the consciousness of human beings and that of the Cosmos in general.

KNOWLEDGE OF THE PLANETS
IN A CONSCIOUSNESS CONTEXT

When I was young, I spent a great deal of time learning about astrology and I acquired so much professional knowledge in the astrological sphere that I could almost interpret horoscopes in my sleep.

Back then, I never thought that, one day, I would get to use my knowledge in a completely different way from most other astrologers, that is to say purely within the context of consciousness.

Nowadays, I know that a horoscope acts primarily as a personal map, indicating certain guidelines for our physical lives here on Earth on a soul level. The principles underlying the actual interpretation are taken directly from the respective planets that are taken into account when interpreting the horoscope.

Everything around us here on Earth and all our human behaviour patterns often originated on one or more of the planets in our solar system.

Today, I know that one of the main objectives of *many* people's lives here on Earth is to integrate energies from other planets in the solar system and in some cases from planets outside this solar system. Furthermore, *everybody* needs to integrate spiritual materialisation power and structure from Earth, so that we can retain our 'newly acquired' energies and knowledge. This is so that when we eventually move back further out into the Cosmos, to our place of origin or home planet or if we come back to be born again on Earth, we will be able to use these things in our future lives and for the evolution of our consciousnesses.

If our energy and insight is not stored in our consciousnesses in a way that makes it possible for us to retain it in our future consciousnesses, no matter where we are heading in the Cosmos, we will not be able to use them anywhere else other than here on Earth. In fact, those insights into consciousness risk being lost as soon as we leave Earth's energy field to be prepared for our next life. We could perhaps imagine that this is the reason why some people here on Planet Earth die of diseases, as they leave the Earth with an imbalance of energy that they will have to deal with on the other side. This enables them to evolve further as basically it makes it possible for them to remember where they have just come from and what experiences of the earthly system they have brought with them.

The knowledge we have here on Earth can come from many different sources. It can be integrated partly through our frequenting of other people and cultures, as well as through education, being in a couple, relationships, parenting, friendships, leisure interests, work, research, technological and societal development, our community and the global environment but also through nature, conflict and war.

The aim of all life in this solar system is to promote comprehensive integration and greater cooperation between the respective planets of our solar system in order to preserve the purest, highest frequencies as well as the most constructive and insightful energies and then to spread them out to all the planets within our solar system. It is here that Planet Earth has a very central role, being the epicentre of this whole integration process.

Furthermore, the goal is also the definitive elimination of any inappropriate or negative energies within the solar system, so that cosmic and indeed overall balance can come about between the planets, for the benefit of both the solar system and the Cosmos as a whole.

When, at some point in the future, our solar system emerges as a unit of combined consciousnesses, we will continue to work together to unite with other solar systems out in other nearer universes and then out into the Cosmos. We have a very long and exciting journey ahead of us and the eventual integration process out there will take place according to the very same principles that we are currently using in our own solar system.

THE PLANETS IN OUR SOLAR SYSTEM

To better understand Earth's role in the overall cosmic development, as well as in our own solar system, I will examine the ten planets in our solar system as well as their influence on consciousness on Planet Earth and on the people and animals that are born with particular planetary influences. As you become acquainted with the basic energies of the planets and their life forms, it will become increasingly easy for you to understand the various energy connections in the solar system. You can also see why it is so difficult to get the overall evolutional cooperation to function in a balanced way!

I shall then review the Crystal energy, which has been integrating more and more powerfully on Earth since 2000, firstly in the auras of all the newly born children and later in the bodies of many children, young people and adults who have a healthy and conscious lifestyle. Body crystallisation can also come about through physical training and I will elaborate on this point later in the book.

Crystal energy can also be found in the auras of all the adults who have had an AuraTransformation™, which you can read about on **www.auratransformation.com**.

Finally, I will review Earth's creation and creative energy and explain how it will affect everyone on the soul and spirit levels, now and in the future, depending on where they are in terms of consciousness.

So buckle up and enjoy the ride as it is now time to get to know a range of different energies which you can only meet in a very pure form, on the level of your imagination, here on Earth.

THE SUN

From a purely energetic point of view, the Sun is a very hot planet with a masculine, burning exterior and a feminine, cold and very conscious core, that, naturally enough, cannot be seen from the outside.

The Sun's energetic structure is the complete opposite of Earth's original energy structure, which previously had a very feminine shell and surface and an equally strong, masculine, burning core. This is an energy relationship that will become increasingly balanced in the future, so that in the long term it will be neither too cold nor too hot anywhere on this planet.

Sun people's life conditions on Earth will improve with every year that passes, whereas they previously felt that it was a torture to be born on this planet, because the energies on Earth's surface were the total opposite of what they knew from home.

Now, Sun people can relax more internally and slowly begin to open up to the other planetary energies that they need to integrate during life here on Earth. When it comes to integration, Sun people still have a lot to learn, as they are originally very clean in their energy but not particularly nuanced.

Being highly egocentric and self-centered has often been associated with the Sun's energy at every level. It is therefore no wonder, that in an astrological interpretation, the Sun's position in the horoscope has always been related directly to the ego and the personality, even though a person with a big personality is not always egocentric.

However, on the Sun, ego and personality have always been very strongly linked to each other. God's power has therefore been aware that if integration is ever going to happen between the basic energies of the ten planets in our solar system, then all the Sun people will have to be really taken down a peg or two on the consciousness level at least once during terrestrial life, in order to root out the deeply ingrained egocentrism and self-centeredness.

Of course Sun people can shine strongly and dazzle other people and warm up their environment to bring about major human achievements. However, what good is that if the energy is only delivered on their terms and when they feel like it and not when there is an absolute need for it? Too much time and energy gets wasted in this way, when in fact, more time and energy needs to be used to coordinate the troops into cooperating than they actually need to get the job done.

This is something that Sun people can easily see for themselves when they want to but which they do not always consider worth doing something about if they do not want to. They are, in fact, totally indifferent to what those around them think once they have decided to go against the current. On the other hand, they will at other times, do anything to follow the current, if they feel it would be advantageous for their very autonomous energy systems.

The Sun has always had very strong pioneering energy, which can partly be seen in the planet's radiance that lights up far out into the solar system, something that the other planets do not do.

It is the Sun's radiance that helps to light up the Moon in relation to Earth and also gives light to other nearby planets. Mercury in particular is strongly influenced by the Sun's light on one hemisphere, while its other hemisphere lies in total darkness.

If Sun people don't have a burning passion about something in their terrestrial lives, they become completely stuck and lose all their power just as when the Sun suddenly disappears behind clouds in the sky. On the Sun, they do not do anything by halves!

Many Sun people can drink black coffee and alcohol, smoke or take pills in huge quantities that would kill anyone with another basic energy. They don't use these stimulants to get high but to soothe the powerless feeling they often get from having been dumped in a very heavy, dense atmosphere here on Planet Earth. Earth's atmosphere and energy structure require their full focus for them to be capable of succeeding in their lives at all. Lack of concentration, focus and hedonism are among the most common reasons why some Sun people are not able to succeed especially well in a terrestrial context. However, they can be capable of enormous success, having the Midas touch as they do.

They would much rather enjoy themselves – by going to a café or a restaurant, enjoying a drink and being with people who can validate their brilliance – than work hard. They tend to believe that it is too much like hard work to have to use their bodies unless they can get some physical pleasure out of it.

Earth represents a heavy energy combination that was not previously comfortable for Sun people to get close to. Consequently, many Sun people have thus far had great resistance to getting involved in the overall integration work here on Earth. They have in fact felt that they were far superior to many of the other planetary energies.

As well as their egocentric energy and the very great involvement in things that have Sun people's interests at heart, they often have a very choleric temperament but you will have to get to know them well to be allowed to witness this at close range. Their fiery temperament is clearly apparent on virtually all fronts if they feel under pressure and then it is best to keep your distance unless you really enjoy a spot of bother. When pressurised, Sun people can no longer keep up appearances, which they are otherwise masters at doing.

Many actors and entertainers come from the Sun, where eternal youth, irresponsibility and being able to sell themselves, as well as mimic those around them, are very distinct behavioural characteristics.

That part of the gay culture that is not necessarily sexually conditioned but where the relationship between two men exists primarily on a comradely, casual and playful basis also belongs to the Sun. In this way, the men involved avoid having to feel really adult and responsible and they also avoid being devoured by women who would emotionally eat them, skin and all.

In this way, things never get really serious and they choose quite deliberately to always keep a back door open in their lives – even on the sexual front – as that is usually the one they choose to make use of when they have sex with each other. That way, the energy doesn't feel so confrontational because, at the moment of release, they avoid having to look the other party in the eye.

Many Sun people often live active lives in the terrestrial context because they find it hard to keep still; they therefore live with a high risk of burning out and dying early. However, if they have many positive things with which to occupy themselves throughout their lives, they can live to a ripe old age.

Many people may be surprised to learn that the Sun has come so far in the overall integration process that it has even initiated a collaborative project with the Moon in our solar system. It is, in fact, possible to appeal to the great humanity of Sun people and luckily, Moon people understood this a long time ago.

Moon people usually find it very difficult to surrender completely to life or to anything outside of themselves, apart from their children. They often cannot work out how to have fun properly. This may be said to be the perfect project for a Sun person to get enthusiastic about.

In this way, many Sun people have voluntarily undertaken the major task of helping Moon people in their personal development, partly with a view to helping them be more spontaneous and happy with life and also to finding more meaning in their lives. In return, Sun people expect Moon people to be deeply grateful to them for all they have done. This does not always happen, however, because Moon people find it very hard to be grateful. This can then spell trouble because Sun people can react very fiercely and from one moment to the next, they completely close off their otherwise warm feelings for Moon people, who often do not have a clue what is going on.

Moon people tend to believe that Sun people are most comfortable with them keeping a low profile. Sun people however, feel that the Moon people are showing a lack of personal involvement and Sun people just cannot bear lack of personal involvement.

I am sure that you now appreciate how difficult it can be for the various planetary energies to understand each other's internal languages. However, God's power succeeded in making the Sun and the Moon follow each other energetically like day and night through hundreds of thousands of years thanks to their joint cooperation with Earth – and so we really can say, so far, so good.

God's power's reward to Sun people for their cooperation with the lunar Energy has partly been to give them luck in life and this makes them feel that they really are something special. Personal benefits and cosmic perks often get Sun people to be extraordinarily industrious without demanding anything in return, simply because they become frivolous and because inwardly they hope that even more goodies will find their towards way to them.

Even though the concepts of alliance and cooperation sound infinitely boring to many Sun people, they are actually the code words for all Sun people to be able to live a positively-evolving life, both here on Earth and back on their home planet.

THE MOON

Millions of years ago, the Moon had a much more materially condensed energy than it has today when there is virtually no condensed energy left on the planet – and in fact, the Moon is not really a planet but a moon, as its name suggests. However, the Moon has the size, power and radiance equivalent to a planet.

All the way back to its origin, the Moon was very materially condensed in its radiance energy and on its surface but it had a liquid core. Earth was the same at its origin, millions of years ago. As time went on however, the Moon gradually became more diffuse and spiritual in its radiance and this from having previously been very inflexible and rigid in its energy on the emotional level. This meant that the Moon always followed the same predictable biorhythms, which unfortunately didn't allow for any rapidly expanding evolution on the consciousness level.

The Moon's development roughly corresponds to that of the Earth's, during millions of years up until the mid-1980s, when there was a sudden end to the upgrading of the soul energy in we humans here on Earth. Instead, it was time for as many people as possible to integrate the spirit energy, which is why Earth now finds itself mainly on the spirit level behind the scenes. It is here that the condensed materialisation power has begun cooperating with the spirit energy in order to better materialise the growing amount of spirit energy on Planet Earth and to make it visible. This heightens Earth's frequency on the surface of the planet where we humans live and one day it will finally match the finely vibrating high-frequency creation energy found deep in the Earth's inner core. However, Earth's consciousness development story is somewhat different from that of the Moon.

The Moon was originally the home of indigenous peoples and

mythical creatures who belonged to the old Earth and to the past. However, since there is no longer materially condensed energy on the Moon, these creatures have been transferred to other planets in the solar system to continue to evolve. Many indigenous peoples have thus continued the development of their consciousnesses under Saturn's guidance here on Earth, where they have been able to live on in much the same way as before but with greater focus on the external framework and survival, rather than on basic animal instincts.

Many Moon people have also been transferred to the Sun to learn to be more outgoing, as Moon people are naturally very introverted and non-physically communicative people. Moreover, some of them have been transferred to Uranus, even though cooperation between the Moon and Uranus is more recent. Uranus has the overall responsibility in the solar system for developing and updating the human template, the humanoid, on the physical and mental levels, a template that everyone, including indigenous peoples and non-terrestrial creatures, need to integrate for it to be possible for them to be born as human beings here on Earth.

The imagination and the world of fairy-tales originate from the Moon, since the Moon is the home of the child mind and whimsy as well as all kinds of feelings that we humans can relate to. Unlike the original, heavy energy around the indigenous peoples and the mythical creatures, the imagination relates to the high-frequency light, physical radiation energy which is still on the Moon. There are few people here on Planet Earth who have not experienced being strongly attracted to the Moon's alluring and deep radiance, which is radically different from the radiance of all the other planets in our solar system, apart from the Sun.

Imagination and a great desire to preserve the child mind and the whimsicality in life are, however, phenomena that are rapidly becoming outdated here on Earth. It is, of course natural for children to show childish behaviour. However, it is less acceptable for adults to behave childishly and capriciously.

Moreover, a group of adults with unconscious Moon energy has been finding it very difficult to distinguish between adult and child relationships in terms of which behaviour belongs to which group. These adult Moon people have transgressed their own children's personal boundaries by clinging to them emotionally and making them dependent or even subjecting them to abuse in the form of incest. They have simply not been able to co-exist in an Earth-appropriate way with their children's spiritual purity and innocence, nor have they been able to separate their own spiritual, physical and instinctive needs from one another, due to their lack of earth-style realism.

Moon people have always instinctively preferred to live a life of physical and/or emotional isolation, either alone or with their children and closest relatives. Generally, they have kept themselves very distant from other people and from big cities, because they cannot bear to have other people's energy close to them, unless those people are soul-related at a very deep level.

They have also often wished on the subconscious plane that they could leave Earth so that they could return to their homely, clean, adventurous, high-frequency but often unrealistic introspective energy. This however, cannot happen until they die and thus leave this planet.

∞ ∞ ∞ ∞ ∞ ∞ ∞ ∞ ∞

The Moon was originally home to the soul energy from which the karma system stems. However, as pure spirit energy is about to occupy Earth in a major way, the Moon and soul energies no longer have any reason to be here. With the gradual arrival on Earth of the Indigo energies back in the mid-1980s (in the auras of all newly-born children), the Moon began slowly slipping out of the general integration effort in our solar system and in around 2000, it became permanently attached to another solar system on the consciousness level. On the physical radiation level, the Moon was and still is, fully visible in our solar system - but as I said earlier, purely energetically it no longer belongs here.

When the Indigo energy came to Earth in 1995 and in the following years, when all babies were born with an Indigo aura instead of a soul aura, astronomers and scientists worldwide interestingly enough began to report that the Moon was in the process of physically moving away from the Earth, the centre of cooperation for development and integration in our solar system. This may well explain why there are no longer any children being born with pure Moon energy here on Earth.

When soul energy is no longer being upgraded in people's auras on this planet, there is no point in letting Moon people come here, as they truly belong on the soul level. They would not feel at home and therefore cannot be a part of the future terrestrial cooperation on the spirit plane. They have integrated high-frequency spirit energy into their energy systems but it is a different type of spirit energy, one that is less material and creative in its structure than the one we are in the process of integrating here on Earth today.

When the Crystal-spirit energy came to Earth from 2004 (every baby was born with a Crystal aura), and from 2009 (all children were born with a Crystal aura and crystallised body energy), people with strong Moon energy found it really difficult to maintain the pace on the bodily and mental levels.

Many adults with strong links to the soul part of the Moon energy

– the less spiritual part – suddenly felt as if an attempt was being made to pull their consciousnesses away from Planet Earth. They could no longer think coherently or function in their daily lives. Some got blood clots in the brain or heart, which set them back on a purely consciousness level, or they even began to get dementia. Many more people than usual were diagnosed with cancer, which originally comes from Moon energy, which, in astrological terms, belongs to the sign of Cancer.

The reason for this inability to concentrate and incipient dementia at that time was due to these people's consciousnesses gradually beginning to migrate to another planetary energy contained within the terrestrial context. Here on Earth they are assigned for the rest of their lives unless they decide they want to move to pure Moon energy. If they do that, it will mean that they can no longer find a place among human beings here on Planet Earth. Many of them will therefore waste away consciously or die.

When all the Moon people on this planet eventually die, they will have the possibility of either following their home planet into the new solar system or shifting to other planets in our solar system to continue the development of their consciousness there.

Despite the external circumstances that are unfolding due to the transition of Moon consciousness to another solar system, the Moon will become an integral part of this other solar system that is completely aligned with its basic energy. So, from an overall consciousness perspective, the Moon energy, on the Moon, is now better off than ever before. Those Moon people who still live here on Earth, and who have been hit hard in both their physical and mental balance, will still never be able to come to terms with the way in which life on Earth will play out in the future as Earth begins, in earnest, to combine material energy with pure spirit energy.

Incidentally, in 2014 as I write this book, the connection between the Moon and all life on Earth has finally been shut down, so there is no longer any consciousness support or possible upgrades to download on the soul level for anyone on Planet Earth. The only way we can get to experience the Moon in the future is to look up in the sky at night, or by physically travelling there.

All Moon people and people on a soul level will now either stay where they are, or will be downgraded in their consciousnesses, so they will not be able to do anything other than follow their predetermined destinies in life. Alternatively, they may choose to have their personal consciousness upgraded to the spirit level. This can be done by having an AuraTransformation™, which is a consciousness transformation method and an upgrading of the aura in adults. I personally helped to bring this method through to Earth back in 1996 and many people, especially in Northern Europe, have already taken the opportunity to upgrade their auras, first to Indigo energy and nowadays to Crystal energy. It means that they have completely left their soul energy behind.

Connect to **www.auratransformation.com** for further information. Other consciousness transformation methods do exist but I am not familiar with them.

∞ ∞ ∞ ∞ ∞ ∞ ∞ ∞ ∞

Pure Moon people are so convinced that they are the crème de la crème in every context that they believe they are totally indispensable. They completely forget that in a terrestrial context they are only periodically visible due to the presence of the Sun energy in their personal energy structure, just as the Moon is only periodically visible in the evening and the night sky because of it reflecting the Sun's light, which it does most strongly at the full moon.

With the Moon's 'disappearance' from the solar system, the desire of human beings to have an all-embracing mother in their lives – a mother who can take full responsibility for their conduct and who helps to maintain the inner child in all adults – has disappeared. This is a really positive thing that has meant that more independent children, who do not risk being tied to their mother's apron strings their entire lives, are now being born here on Earth.

Furthermore, heterosexual and lesbian relationships based purely on being immersed in the emotions rather than on sexual attraction are on the verge of disappearing. In fact, the parties involved have often experienced these relationships as extremely transgressive, since these parties – principally Moon women – have often tried to penetrate deeper into their partner's inner being and energy than they have been able to do in their own energies and much deeper than it would ever become possible to penetrate a man's energy system.

This means that soon, nobody on Earth will be able to trespass on another's intimate sphere, at an emotional level, in the body. This will mean that it will become impossible to control a partner's body using emotions. This is because the individual's energy must at all costs be preserved here on Earth until the day, far into the future, when we will have progressed so far in the development of our consciousnesses that each of us will merge with the supreme cosmic force, the place of unitary energy.

∞ ∞ ∞ ∞ ∞ ∞ ∞ ∞ ∞

Many people on Planet Earth have had strong links to each other on the consciousness level because of the Moon's presence in our solar system. The reason for this is that numerous agreements were entered into on the soul level to support each other energetically in everything, because up until now, the Moon was the seat of soul energy.

These agreements however, were entered into in a sphere where the energy was significantly more diffuse and soul-related compared to the less condensed energy here on Earth. It is therefore difficult to draw direct parallels between the two energy spheres of the Moon and Earth. Many people have therefore evolved in a different direction from that originally anticipated when they first came to Earth with Moon energy in their personal consciousnesses. Therefore, they no longer have such close soul connections with others as they used to experience in the pure Moon energy.

This means that people with varying degrees of Moon energy in their system no longer have a soul-related backing group to help them stay extra strong in their personal radiance and consciousness, or in their bodies, if they don't take care of themselves. There is no longer any dear Moon mother protecting them on an energy level when they do something wrong. No matter where we come from energetically, everyone on Earth at this time needs to be individualised on the personal level, so that they can learn to stand strongly in their own energy.

No one else can, or should, take responsibility for anyone else's actions and no one else is expected to stand behind the scenes to assist anyone energetically if they do not make an effort to do it themselves. These are the terms on the spirit level, for anyone who wants to live a conscious life on the Crystal level on Earth, as we transition to the Golden energy. In the Golden era no one is permitted to continue to live totally unconsciously; Earth is an extremely conscious and intelligent planet and at this time full focus is on making everyone conscious and aware at different levels and in different areas.

No one is allowed to take part in terrestrial development if they do not individually contribute something positive to the Whole, whether it is to their children, grandchildren or other relatives, friends, acquaintances, neighbours, community or their country. However, it is important to point out that what is perceived as positive in one country is not always seen as positive in another. We have not yet got that far in Earth's development, or that of the solar system, that every country has the same set of values and rules of conduct. This will happen at a later stage in the development of consciousness and the integration process.

So even if many people had a feeling of being spiritually connected when living at soul level here on Earth, today the situation is somewhat different. Now people must instead learn how to connect with each other on all levels and not just in spirit.

MERCURY

Every astrologer knows that the planet Mercury is related to communication. On Mercury, however, they do not communicate with speech; they communicate with mental energy and the transfer of brain oscillations and frequencies to reach a common understanding of the correlation of things. This doesn't mean, however, that Mercury people like to socialise and share their inner thoughts with others. They do not. Not even with their 'closest' friends.

Mercury is an energy that is continually informing itself about what others are doing and how they are doing it and why they are doing it. Here on Earth, this kind of knowledge-related update takes place principally through research, the internet, books, magazines and newspapers, as well as through written communication, so you can show where you have acquired your knowledge.

There is also a strong focus on conversation and on-going status updates, both on the phone and on social media, which could sometimes be classified as gossip, as not everything is retransmitted as it is received. This is because the Mercury energy has periodic 'outages' in its memory, often caused by stress. If, however, the Mercury person is in balance, their memory will be excellent, meaning that everything will be correctly retransmitted down to the very last detail.

On the sunny side of Mercury, which is a very short distance from the Sun, there is a strong and sometimes extremely powerful, ultraviolet light. Mercury people from that side of the planet are therefore often strongly attracted to the Sun's rays and/or sunbeds during their time here on Earth. On the other hand, it is extremely cold on the dark hemisphere of the planet, where very few things are able to survive.

The dark hemisphere of Mercury represents a form of mental anti-energy, as it resembles a big black hole in the consciousness if you get too close to this energy. The anti-energy represents the void which can arise in consciousness when you no longer have anything to do in life and when there is no more burning passion or anything to talk about.

Mental anti-energy is characterised by the empty depressive state that takes over when light and movement leave a human to be replaced by darkness and stagnation.

On Mercury, a very strong mental communication net has been developed from which we benefit greatly here on Planet Earth, where the energy has taken the form of telephone, communication and computer systems and the like. On Mercury, there is a lot of theoretical and practical know-how on many fronts.

There is, however, one major shortcoming on the planet - there is no heart energy, which is why the Mercurians have had to ally themselves with their neighbouring planet Venus to open up this aspect of consciousness in their energy systems. It is not possible to multiply quickly enough on the planet using only logic and a great understanding of correlation when working according to the integration conditions that apply to the entire solar system. Mercury is therefore becoming relatively depopulated in comparison with its large populations of previous times.

This is partly because, over the last millennia, many Mercury people have emigrated from their home planet because they have had a strong sense of lacking something essential in their lives and they have often sought in the direction of Venus to enable love-intelligent energy to be integrated into their systems.

Another explanation for the depopulation of Mercury is that many Mercury people choose not to have children, or perhaps they are partially sterile. Here on Earth, Mercury people may be sterile or childless, due to various external factors in their lives such as working conditions and hours and possible radiation hazards or other risks related to their jobs. It may also be because they fail to meet the right partner while they are of child-bearing age. Many Mercury people also find it difficult to give themselves completely to life and to love with a partner. They feel that they are losing control and feel emotionally vulnerable as soon as they try to involve their heart in relation to another adult.

Mercury people always have their antennae up and are very open to new input and any new ideas. They are therefore quick to grasp that there are many other more exciting and rewarding ways of doing things out and about in the solar system than those they have already learned.

To be fair, they are very helpful to their fellow human beings, even though they don't always have sufficient internal and/or human resources to be truly useful. They often try to help other people because they want to be friendly, as they have so much understanding regarding everyone and everything – especially about problems – which they very much want to help solve, maybe because they hope that the heart energy will thus grow in their consciousnesses. However, on the energetic level, that is not how things work.

A desire to help others must come from the heart, because you feel it, not because it is what is expected of you. When the heart energy has been integrated at some point in the consciousnesses of all Mercury people, it will not be at all difficult for them to understand that you can often help people better by saying no, rather than only being able to help them in half measures.

Mercury people mostly surround themselves with things that are simple, stylish and of high quality and everything is always clean and tidy around them. However, there is little charm or character to be found in their surroundings.

VENUS

The master energy and the Crystal energy, which belong to Venus, represent, together with Earth's inner Golden creation and creative force, the highest-frequency energy of all in our solar system. In fact, the energy of Venus is of such a high frequency that it has taken thousands of years for it to be fully grasped by people here on Earth.

The Crystal energy first came fully to Earth at the beginning of 2009 and it is important to understand that the Crystal energy spoken of here is the variant that manifests itself in our solar system. Around the Cosmos, there are actually several other variants but they are not able to materialise in the same visible way in the terrestrial sphere as Venus Crystal energy, quite simply because they are not a part of the spiritual-material cooperation taking place here on Planet Earth and on all the planets in our solar system.

Consequently, many spiritual people who are attracted to various lighter forms of Crystal energy that come from different places outside our solar system can find it very difficult to convert the Crystal energy into a form that everyone can relate to on the visible human and material level. They can often only make contact with the Crystal energy by meditating, or when they are in a dream-rich, REM sleep state.

Most incarnated high-frequency Venus people and Venus masters have been perceived, for many millennia, as very cynical, blunt, ruthless, rigid managerial types. Many ordinary people have wanted to follow them but at the same time, they have been afraid to consult with them because they could not bear to hear the truth. They have therefore not been able to pick up on the vast, humanly all-embracing love-intelligence, which has always been hidden behind the wise and truthful words of Venus people.

Many other planet types have been able to say exactly the same things as Venus people without being met with resistance, because they tend to express things in much lower, deeper, lower-frequency energies which ordinary people have been able to grasp. Venus people often hit the spot so well when they express themselves on a given matter that they do not always know themselves how close to the truth they are; a trait that often means that high-frequency Venus people appear to be almost superhuman and psychic to those around them.

It is not really so surprising that many spiritually conscious Venus people have had this effect on those around them when you consider that there is very high-frequency spiritual energy and very little physical energy on Venus and no terrestrial con-densed energy at all. Consequently, it took a very long time for high-frequency Venus people to land with their feet firmly down on Earth. Of course, this is no longer a problem for them as the Crystal energy is now part of all newly born children's auras and is no longer a threatening or unattainable energy.

It usually takes a while before Venus people understand and accept the terrestrial rules of the game when they first come to Earth but once they have learned them, they cannot be tricked anymore. They then start to give back to those around them some of the same stuff that these people have been sending out but in a respectful and loving way. However, if they feel bruised by an experience they will shut off completely.

Venus people are often very clear and bright in their radiance and appearance, a look that through the centuries has been coveted and imitated in the worst possible manner by several of the other planetary energies. This has happened in the hope that they might succeed in integrating the high-frequency Venus energy. This is part of the reason why many women, the world over, bleach their hair.

Venus is referred to by many as Earth's 'sister planet' and as both the morning star and the evening star, as you can often see it as a very bright star in the morning sky just before sunrise and in the evening sky just after sunset.

The air is very clean on Venus, although the atmosphere seems damp and misty, just like a greenhouse. There is actually a very dense and inaccessible layer of clouds at an altitude of 50-80 km surrounding the entire planet; this consists of sulphur dioxide and sulphuric acid. This layer of cloud is roughly similar to the Venus people's auras and radiance, which is not always easy to see through either. However, when others are able to see and accommodate the energy of Venus people as it truly is, the obscuring haze disappears immediately.

Venus is a planet controlled purely by consciousness, where everything you see on the outside corresponds exactly to the internal energetic state of every Venus person; this is a highly intelligent and fascinating energy system that is infinitely difficult to see through for those around it, but where all Venus people feel at home. This is how they are able to protect their direct access to God's power from being abused by other planetary energies, which often operate on lower energy frequencies than those of Venus.

People with low-frequency energies generally don't understand the concept of spiritual balance. They often want to use God's power to their own personal ends, which is in direct contrast to Venus people's attitude to life.

Camouflage and opacity are often precious qualities when it comes to safeguarding a great capacity to see clearly and focus.

These are qualities that many Venus people possess without it necessarily being visible and/or comprehensible to those around them. Since Venus represents the highest love-intelligence of all in our solar system, the objective of its energy is love-intelligent balance and balance in general, not greed and selfishness.

When it comes to love, what matters is precisely the ability to focus energy in a very specific direction, so that it does not disperse and risk being lost somewhere.

Because of the eternal presence of balance on Venus, there has always existed, as part of the love intelligence, a form of intelligent realism, which is a very mental and controlled version of love and which acts as a counterbalance. We could describe this as 'intelligent love'. So even if it is hard for many people to understand, the presence of hardness and realism on Venus are quite clearly justified, also and especially, in the lives of Venus people here on Earth.

On Planet Earth, it is often an advantage to be able to set boundaries and cut through to the bone in certain situations without getting carried away by emotions. If evolution on this planet were only a question of focusing on love and balance, precious few would use their resources to contribute to the overall social development. People would risk being lazy in the name of love and hardness and realism, among other things, are needed to cut through this and order people to get back to work.

Hardness and acceptance of reality are also needed when people are seriously ill and about to die and you have to let them go for their own good. It thus requires a lot of courage and a correspondingly high level of consciousness to dare to be efficient at solving problems and providing an overall balance.

All Venus people who are not at master level and who have a

more physical than spiritual approach to life generally find that it is always best to choose balance in every area of life. They rarely get involved in anything without having a guarantee of a successful outcome. The more ordinary Venus people clearly belong to the rank and file in life, which very spiritually conscious Venus masters most definitely do not. A master would never imagine wearing a safety vest because they are afraid of dying. If the time has come for them to depart this Earth, they know it deep inside themselves and nothing can save them from dying.

If conscious Venus people feel danger, they will choose to take a different route but they will rarely stay at home if help is needed elsewhere.

MARS

Mars was originally home to the four basic elements - earth, water, fire and air in our solar system.

At the start of the solar system, these four elements were co-ordinated and controlled exclusively from Mars and converted into energy with very different and powerful forms of expression, such as wind, lightning, thunder, waves, undercurrents in water and so on.

Today, Venus is in charge of the overall control and coordination of the four elements in our solar system, as Venus represents a much higher frequency and is a far more balanced energy and form of expression than Mars. However, at the end of the Mayan calendar in December 2012, responsibility for the further development and utilisation of the four elements on Planet Earth was handed over to Earth itself.

Many thousands of years ago, Venus became responsible for the elements' ways of expressing themselves in our solar system because Mars, more or less voluntarily, chose to submit to the balanced way Venus handles life. The alternative for Mars would have been to continue to follow the far more reptilian and primitively simple development path that characterised the planet's energy in ancient times.

These days, Mars people and people strongly influenced by Mars energy are no longer allowed to live a loveless, unconscious life with no regard for others, without it having serious human consequences for them.

An outward sign that love was originally lacking on Mars is that almost all of their living creatures are very ugly and of primitive appearance. This is seen especially clearly in the animals that have their origins on the planet, such as iguanas, large tortoises, lizards, cold-water fish and others. Mars is undoubtedly the most unattractive planet in our solar system.

Many Mars people are not particularly attractive in appearance in conventional terms, as they may have very indelicate facial and/ or body features, often looking scarred and worn out at an early age. The old Vikings came from Mars and many Mexicans and Latin Americans with war in their blood also have their energetic source from this planet. These days, anyone whose reflex is to pull out a knife when they disagree with others, rather than sit down and talk constructively about the issue, clearly has Mars energy in their system, as does anyone who starts a fight without being provoked just for the 'fun' of it. Many Mars people actually have a personal on-off switch well hidden in their energy system, which can cause them to ignite spontaneously and attack other people if they are bored and have nothing else to do, or if for some reason they do not like somebody. You should therefore not joke about a Mars person's fiery temperament, as you run the risk of suddenly becoming a victim of their uncontrolled anger and aggression.

In fact, it is almost impossible to imagine how bad things could have got if Venus had not assumed primary responsibility for the four elements in our solar system and for the future conscious-ness development of Mars as an integral part of the solar system.

An example of the original inhumanity of Mars people can be seen in the utterly barbaric disaster that took place in and around Germany during the 2nd World War:

Since many Venus people are very light-skinned, blonde and typically Northern European in appearance, it did not take long for Hitler and his cronies, who mainly consisted of primitive-thinking Mars people, to figure out that the breeding of the perfect human being (the Aryan race) had to be the ultimate solution for them to create and develop the Venus energy in a physical form on Earth. The goal was thus for them to 'produce' Venus energy and Venus people in a physical form by 'cutting and pasting' body parts from selected test subjects and prisoners who were forced to participate in these experiments.

Trading and theft of human organs has never been alien to the Mars energy. On the contrary, it seems very natural for this energy to recycle other people's bodily and material possessions as if they had always been their own.

The problem with Hitler's insane plan was that the very physically-focused Mars energy mistakenly thought that the Venus energy could be brought into being by making physical adjustments to the body and by brainwashing people to think positively. The people behind him simply didn't understand that Venus energy represents an inner balanced state that cannot be nurtured by the use of external force or war. They tried to cut corners by killing a very large group of people on Planet Earth who did not fit into their ideal image of what a perfect Venus person looked like. The main purpose was to experiment, here on Earth, to see if it was possible for them to create the Venus energy in a physical form, meaning that they would no longer need to be subjected to Venus's control of their energy at home on Mars.

This was a truly horrific plan completely devoid of heart energy; these actions can never be excused.

The huge quantities of people who died in the pursuit of 'the perfect human being' were not something that would weigh heavily on Mars's conscience. They knew that the Venus energy is divine and mostly unattainable for ordinary people, because its energy emits such high frequencies. So what would it matter in the overall energy reckoning whether here on Earth two, three or five million lives had to be sacrificed to take a short-cut to integrate this divine energy for the benefit of its own people on the home planet?

There is a lot more to this gruesome story which I will not go into here but I am sure that most people will agree that it was not from the supreme power of God that Nazi Germany derived its inspiration when it thought up such heinous things. In fact, every energetic trick in the book was used to clarify how this self-created Venus integration and human cleansing project could take place in the most productive and efficient way. Many seers and clairvoyant advisers were consulted in connection with the project because Mars people love to get a glimpse of the future and to peer into the lives of others, so they can anticipate the next move for their own benefit. Mars people love competition and most of all they love winning, often demeaning and humiliating the loser very publicly.

Similar events have unfortunately occurred in South America where Chile and Argentina in particular have been influenced by the Mars energy, which is also very well represented in Mexico. It was, of course, to these countries that many senior Nazis fled after the 2nd World War.

∞ ∞ ∞ ∞ ∞ ∞ ∞ ∞ ∞

Many Mars people are extremely self-promoting and they don't usually help others until their irritation at the state of things exceeds their own selfishness, laziness and needs. If they are feeling helpful and there is no one around them who they can help in a way that suits them, they will create their own victims by hurting them or trying to make them weak. Similarly, they are very quick to assign themselves the leading role in any situation if they are not completely satisfied with the role that other people may have given them.

In truth, Mars energy has never been extraordinary on account of something that the energy itself has created but even so, everything is always about comparing themselves to those around them. Life is therefore a series of victories over other people, while they choose, of course, to ignore their defeats, unless they decide to get revenge.

Many Mars people often get pleasure from the downfall of others without even being aware of it. Consequently, they have no problem stealing or 'borrowing' from other people if they are missing something whether it be energy, human reserves or material values. It will therefore come as no surprise to anyone that property crime and the serpent in the Garden of Eden, with its voice of temptation, originated from Mars.

The serpent tempts its prey, toys with it and finally devours every scrap of it. It then feels pleasantly full and satisfied. Most Mars people feel like this when they have eaten, drunk alcohol in large quantities and had sex. You can almost see the serpent in front of you with a huge bulging stomach as the prey is being digested. Similarly, it is not difficult to spot a newly satisfied and extremely contented Mars person.

Since everything is coherent on the pure energetic plane at all levels in our solar system and the majority of all snakes, lizards and other sensory species come from Mars, these animals' characteristics are very strongly associated with the planet's energetic appearance, which is also reflected in Mars people's behaviour here on Earth.

Mars people have always been very extrovert out and about in the solar system, where they go on the prowl, sneaking around after something that they can consume or spend their time and energy on. They often set themselves very specific physical goals, where the end result can be financial gain or the slaughter of a whole town, using brutality and rape to show off their physical dominance. They have therefore tried to invade their neighbouring planets in the solar system several times, just as the Vikings did in various countries, just to be able to go pillaging.

It is not only alien planets that the Mars energy tends to invade. On Earth and on the other planets in the solar system, Mars people are constantly trying to gnaw their way into other people's consciousness in the hope of stealing energy from them. Now that Planet Earth's Golden creation and creative force, in co-operation with the Venus Crystal energy, have taken control of Earth's energy, it will become really difficult for Mars people to steal energy from others.

When the Venus Crystal energy is in play, people copy the best of each other to subsequently integrate those copied energies into their own consciousness systems in a balanced way. However, this requires that you are able to master the particular energies for yourself in a positive and balanced way; if you cannot, you have to start all over again.

The larger goal of a close encounter between Mars and Venus, in a terrestrial context, was originally that all Mars people should fully integrate the love-intelligence into their consciousnesses. Unfortunately, it appears that the majority of Mars people do not really want to integrate the Venus energy in a completely pure form. They would much rather suck all the nutrients out of Venus for their own personal benefit, which is a direct repudiation of the larger plan from God's power for our solar system.

As a consequence of the thieving behaviour of the Mars energy,

God's power, in connection with the start of 'The New Earth' on 21 December 2012, decided to separate the Mars energy from that of Venus. Consequently, the Mars energy will have to learn by itself to recognise its human and energetic deficiencies by comparing itself with the other residents of the solar system.

Mars people will thus be left to live with their own energetic errors and deficiencies on the development level where each is located; that is to say, where they have chosen to be with their varying degrees of camouflaged selfishness and egocentrism.

∞ ∞ ∞ ∞ ∞ ∞ ∞ ∞ ∞

Mars people are very goal-oriented and task-oriented by nature. They only show flexibility and adaptability if they feel that their opponent is invincible. They are therefore extremely focused on the use of titles where it is visible to everyone who is 'the boss' and has earned the right to be, and who are 'subordinates'.

Mars people like to be the ones making the decisions and it feels quite natural for them to manage and distribute tasks, as well as have other people working under them. Therefore it also feels natural for them to have strangers both to care for their children and to relieve them sexually. Prostitution and the trafficking of human bodies for many different purposes, as well as meeting other people's needs in return for payment, is actually just as natural for them as life itself. Fortunately, the presence of the Venus energy in many Mars peoples' lives has led them to become more aware of the presence of love in their lives than before.

The Ashtar Command, or our solar system's warriors, belongs in the highest frequencies of Mars, very close to Venus. However, there are also a number of other Ashtar Commands outside the solar system (which I will not go into here). The very power-ful Ashtar-Mars warriors, who are some very bright, almost blinding, war-like creatures, were often sent off to Earth in the past to support people in remaining strong in their faith on the mental level if they had had really bad experiences or abuse in their physical lives.

However, the Ashtar Command has not always managed to tackle rescue tasks in the same love-intelligent way that the Venus energy would have done in similar situations. When the Ashtar Command, through its spiritual guidance, has tried to influence distressed people on the mental level to get on with their lives in the best way, the Ashtar warriors have, in many cases, been adversely affected themselves by abusive situations. They have therefore often advised the distressed people to make use of war in the struggle to survive when, in fact, the latter had asked for help from the higher powers. Violent riposte in no way corresponds to the far more balanced approach to life of the Venus energy. If all parties continue making war against one another, it will be absolutely impossible to integrate the best planetary qualities from one another and live in balance here on Earth.

Many Ashtar warriors, far back in history when the Earth's energy seemed outwardly very heavy and soulless, were taken prisoner and trapped in the heaviest part of the Earth's energy sphere without being able to get back to their home planet. This is because they had fallen so heavily in energy frequency that they had not been able to move back up into the highest-frequency Mars energies close to Venus. When all of these warriors are set free from Planet Earth's heaviest energy sphere, which will happen from 2016 onwards when the Pleiadian energy really takes its rightful divine place on Earth, we will notice a major positive heightening of Earth's overall energy frequencies for the benefit of all.

You can read about the Pleiadian energy, which is the energy

of the angels of God and not a part of our solar system, later in
the book.

JUPITER

All people here on Earth who have a very strong connection in their consciousness to Sirius and the Pleiades, regarding their spiritual development, arrived here via either Jupiter or Uranus, as these two planets originally represented the only two gateways in and out of our solar system.

Later, Neptune began to open up contact with the Pleiades and Orion, and the Moon began cooperating with Sirius A, as well as with selected star people who came from the Pleiades, also known as the Seven Sisters.

Last but not least, Venus began communicating directly on a visible level with alien planets, galaxies, solar systems and universes outside our solar system, which was quite normal, since Venus has always acted as a cosmic node, having contact with all existing energies in the entire Cosmos. So it was actually only in our little solar system that we were not aware of this 'behind the scenes' communication that had nonetheless always existed. The overall goal of all this communication between different planets, stars and so on, besides creating balance within our own solar system, was to begin connecting the various solar systems with one another on the consciousness level, so that together they could help to increase the overall consciousness in the liver-universe of which our solar system is a part.

Here on Earth, all direct contact with planets, star clusters and galaxies in the external world to our solar system had always been firmly closed, thereby making it easier to keep control of the solar system's own energies. Consequently, many extraterrestrial beings who have chosen to incarnate in a human body on Planet Earth have often found it very difficult to feel at home in the terrestrial sphere and in their own bodies, since they have been unable to feel their own original energy anywhere.

It was only when the extremely transformative Indigo energy, which has its source on Jupiter, began to stir in the summer of 1987 that people with extra-terrestrial and other different energies began to feel hopeful about one day being able to live joyful and balanced lives on this planet where they would finally be able to begin to truly feel their own basic energy. Up until 1987, many of them had actually had to restrict their large and/or different personal consciousnesses to try to fit into the karma-driven soul energy that had guided all life on the planet for hundreds of thousands of years. So it is actually thanks to the Jupiter energy that many people with extra-terrestrial and other energies now feel at home here on Earth because of the consciousness-transforming initiatives that have emerged since the Indigo energy found its way to Earth.

The Indigo energy, interestingly enough, found its way to Earth via the many children who, from the summer of 1987, were born with varying amounts of Indigo energy in their auras. If an opening were to have been created for the energy through adult human beings working on expanding their own consciousness, the energy would never have been able to come through to Earth so quickly.

Today, extra-planetary creatures are allowed into our solar system but it is only through agreement (a dispensation) with Planet Earth's creative power that a large number of well-balanced and self-sufficient angels with Pleiadian energy started to gain access to Earth via Venus from April 2014. This happens on the understanding that Venus, which represents the highest frequency, most powerful and most balanced energy in our solar system, vouches for the Pleiadian angels who contribute to creating a sustained increase in the frequency on our planet.

However, it is the individual Pleiadian angel's life purpose that determines whether a dispensation is granted for being born on Earth or not.

∞ ∞ ∞ ∞ ∞ ∞ ∞ ∞ ∞

Most Jupiter people who do not have Indigo energy are usually typically early risers who get up in the morning with the Sun and go to bed early in the evening as the Sun disappears, unless they are lured to an exciting party.

It is extremely important for the personal well-being of all Jupiter people that they ensure they keep a fixed daily rhythm, especially if they are to be happy and radiate vitality and personal reserves of energy, in keeping with their planet's basic structure.

Jupiter people are usually very strong and flexible in their bodies and many of them are very tall and proud in appearance, like the Maasai people in Kenya and Tanzania. Unfortunately personal self-indulgence is reflected extremely rapidly in their bodies in the form of overweight.

They are also very enlightened, right-minded, spiritually inquisitive, friendly and attentive by nature. However, they are not particularly loving in their self-expression. They have a lot of humour but are basically hard to get close to, as they protect their personal, intimate spheres intensely, as well as their personal freedom.

Despite their strong desire for freedom and human insight, as well as their great openness, good will and direct way of communicating with the outside world, Jupiter people rarely make a visible fuss outwardly when they are unhappy with something. If those around them are unable to read their dissatisfaction with the state of things, they will quietly shut down their goodwill in relation to the people concerned. It is in this way that Jupiter people see themselves as showing the greatest possible respect in relation to other people and their personal freedom.

Jupiter people will rarely fight for anything other than justice. They do not even fight in their marital relationships.

∞ ∞ ∞ ∞ ∞ ∞ ∞ ∞ ∞

The religious beliefs of Buddhism and Islam originate from Jupiter as a visible means for people to integrate spiritual consciousness into everyday life. As the integration process has gradually progressed in this solar system, Islam has mostly been steered by Pluto in the way it is being practised here on Earth, whereas the faith is still practised in its purest spiritual form in many places on its home planet of Jupiter.

Similarly, Islam is practised in a very high-frequency and spiritual way in several places here on Earth, even though it isn't always reflected as such in the media because of the strong urge of the Pluto energy to use terror in the fight to Islamise and control the world.

The very first planetary cooperation that took place in our solar system, and which had nothing to do with the current integration cooperation programme on Planet Earth, took place between the Sun and Jupiter. It is therefore not surprising that the Buddha, who was the messenger of Buddhism, originally came from the Sun. He was later assigned to Jupiter and is now connected with the Earth's creation and creative power and the work of developing and balancing the New Time Earth.

Buddhism is practised by all kinds of people all over Earth regardless of their planetary background but Sun people feel particularly strongly attracted to this life-affirming faith that is like a heavenly morsel for them, perhaps because the Sun energy originally had a hand in it.

Jupiter is the largest of all the planets in our solar system and it was also the first inhabited planet in our solar system, which is why many concepts and thoughts have emerged from there to be later transferred to other planets in the solar system and beyond.

The Sun and Pluto in particular have been queuing up to receive energetic information from Jupiter regarding their personal spiritual and human development, which have not been particularly advanced on the inner levels.

The Sun and Pluto in their purest forms best understand about external appearance, where everything is exactly as it is appears to be. Jupiter, in turn, is the master of what is within and not just without. Jupiter people therefore generally have a much 'wider-spectrum' outlook and understanding than either Sun or Pluto people. It is therefore not surprising that most lawyers and judges have Jupiter energy.

SATURN

Saturn is a very industrious and destiny-laden planet – at least when it comes to astrological interpretation – and it is known by its very distinctive rings, also called the rings of destiny, which circle the planet and which consist of numerous small ice and rock particles.

Saturn people base their way of life on survival rather than living and enjoying life and they spend most of their time on striving to gain more influence and have a bigger and better material framework in their lives. The higher the seniority and the better the title they have, the greater their *raison d'être* and value to society, they feel.

Saturn people are bereft of even the most basic human and interpersonal needs and values and they devote little time in their lives to sex and feelings. Sex is something you do to procreate to ensure that the family line continues. When it comes to emotions, they can be characterised as being the 'least evolved' beings in the solar system.

They have photographic memories and know many things off by heart after having seen and heard them only once. They like to push everything else aside to acquire fresh knowledge and to learn from other peoples' experiences.

Living in houses and smaller residential buildings on Earth is an idea originally brought here from Saturn. Saturn people, by virtue of their strong urge to constantly strive for more than they already have, have always had a similarly great urge to keep others at a distance in order to preserve their personal knowledge, integrity and intimate sphere.

Looking at their human needs, we could imagine that a small flat in a block ought to fully cover what they appear to need. However, this type of housing does not suit them at all, since Saturn people do not want to have strangers too close to them.

Animal husbandry and self-sufficiency or growing your own food are phenomena that come from Saturn, where, as mentioned earlier, everything is about personal survival.

While they are young, most Saturn people often forego partying and enjoying life as soon as possible in order to get on at work or in sport. They never complain about the personal price they have to pay to succeed early in life.

Later on, things often degenerate for them on a personal level because they have completely forgotten to prioritise family, friendships and close relationships in their lives. So when there is nothing more to strive for, life more or less ends for them. Many Saturn people die shortly after they retire because they no longer have any personal reference points in life beyond their former jobs and titles.

Because of its one-sidedness and lack of spirituality, Saturn energy has today pulled away from the Earth's energy sphere. There are no longer any pure Saturn people being born on this planet but Saturn still has an active role in the solar system, although not in connection with the joint integration process at the human level.

URANUS

On the soul level, many Uranus people, without knowing it with their everyday consciousnesses, have been allotted some of the most demanding tasks in the solar system. They have been strong advocates of advanced technological and industrial development, messengers of the New Age energy and all the alternative thinking and treatments, as well as vegetarianism, animal welfare and all the humanitarian and social initiatives and organisations that have emerged all over Planet Earth. In fact, they have fought for many of the same societal values on the soul level that the spiritually high-frequency Venus Crystal energy is now in the process of developing on the spirit level.

It is interesting, however, that high-frequency spiritual energy has never existed on Uranus, nor is there any terrestrial condensed soul energy or karma to manage the overall development of the planet.

All that exists on Uranus is terrestrial and physically vibrating spirit energy that can be detected with various measuring instruments. The hallmark of this form of energy is that it is always in motion but doesn't always have a specific goal. Consequently, Uranus people here on Earth often end up being resistant when other people try to persuade them to move in a particular direction or to set themselves some specific goals in life. Most of all they want to be independent with no binding ties to other people, animals and places.

Uranus energy, which was first discovered by people here on Earth in 1781 and which therefore only began to affect the lives of soul people on the everyday consciousness level from that time onwards, is our solar system's first system breaker. That is precisely why Uranus people have been very effective in their battle to destroy all old time thinking and all the old consciousness systems here on Earth.

In the summer of 1987, the Uranus energy was followed by the burgeoning Indigo energy that eventually filled the auras of all children who were born between 1995 and 2004. The Indigo energy is not just a system-breaking energy though; it is a resolutely transformative energy that literally turned the world upside down to create the basis for a new type of consciousness.

Uranus people would rather go their own way than follow a trail that others have created. As I have said, they don't like established systems and mind-sets and would much rather fail with something they have created themselves than succeed with something that other people have created. The uncertainty factor and the novelty value are actually far more important to them than succeeding in the usual often predictable and boring way.

If a typical Uranus person has just been through a serious crisis, do not be surprised to hear them say "Why bother with such trivialities? Let's move on!"

Uranus people are extremely quick to speak up if they are unhappy about something. They shout so loudly and often spread such a lot of mental noise around that practically the whole world can hear them. In fact, it is totally impossible for those around them to avoid hearing them.

They love news of all sorts and like to use shock-effects to impress other people, sell their message and convince the world that they are good at what they do, mostly because it confirms to them that their lives are in constant development and that they are able to make a difference in society. However, they tend to want development for development's sake, rather than using existing high-quality methods that have already proved their efficiency.

∞ ∞ ∞ ∞ ∞ ∞ ∞ ∞ ∞

There are two general types of people on Uranus – the development type and the rebellious type.

The development type will have often travelled to alien solar systems, galaxies and universes in the hunt for all things new. They love information and new developments that they can take back home to Uranus, like surfing the internet for news and information. Uranus energy then, is seldom the one which has originally come up with the good ideas. Most ideas are borrowed from elsewhere in the Cosmos, since the Uranus energy has so far travelled further afield than any other energy in our solar system.

Uranus people are very mentally oriented and have an extremely well-developed third eye which they can use in many different dimensions. What they see, however, will depend on the energies with which they have previously fraternised out and about in the Cosmos and which they will have stored in their mental memory for later use.

The rebellious type is often characterised as being a 'true' Uranus person.

For the most part, they have very low-frequency energy that in no way corresponds to their own self-image. They gladly attribute to themselves all kinds of special, unique qualities, that no other person has, because otherwise they are not unique.

Characteristic of both Uranus types is that neither of them has a single drop of heart energy in their consciousness system, unless they have visited their neighbouring planet of Neptune to acquire high-vibrating spiritual energy.

Most Uranus people often want to be different at all costs, whether they belong to the developing or rebellious type. Consequently, there is seldom peace and balance in their lives and it is almost impossible for them to keep the peace with those around them for long periods of time because they get bored rapidly if things become too nice and balanced.

They really need to have something meaningful to fight for in their lives, even if it is just a little trifle that they can turn into a great cause. Uranus people love politics, arguments and discussions and they are almost willing to die for their beliefs and their personal opinions if they consider it necessary.

They therefore have no problem exposing other people to death and violence in the name of a cause, which most other planet types find deeply objectionable. Here it is easy to see that there is a lack of heart energy on Uranus, which unfortunately means that many Uranus people are heartless and totally devoid of compassionate feelings in their lives here on Earth.

On the other hand, they are extremely good at coding computers and human brains, the latter often occurring via telepathy and brainwashing without the victim being aware of it. So even though Uranus people don't have direct contact with each other in everyday life, they can usually easily detect each other's thoughts at a distance; they are in fact masters of telepathy.

Here on Planet Earth, telepathy is often used by Uranus people to control those around them, for example in advertising and the presentation of new products on the market. Uranus people are actually experts in persuading those around them to act in a certain way or to buy certain products through massive exposure and marketing as well as an unconscious encoding of people's consciousness. They know exactly which buttons to press in order to get a particular message across to customers.

Musically, Uranus people understand how to influence the masses and they understand especially well how to influence young Uranus people to behave in a fashionable and rebellious way. Most Uranus music is in fact extremely noisy and loud, containing many unconscious signals often very well camouflaged in both the music and the lyrics.

Taking the two types of people on Uranus as benchmarks, the developing type can primarily be assigned to the technological and consciousness development on Earth, while the rebellious type represents showdowns with the forces of law and order during demonstrations and similar.

These rebels cannot help but make trouble and if, against all expectation, they should happen to adjust to the surrounding community, you can often expect human and/or sexual perversions and aggression, as well as psychopathic traits in their daily behaviour and lifestyle.

Standing out from the masses is simply so deeply ingrained in the personality of all rebellious Uranus people that they can't actually manage to adapt to other people at all. They are too anarchic in their basic structure and therefore many of them in recent years are in the process of being removed from Earth through various natural disasters, wars and riots around the planet.

However, there are great developmental opportunities in store for the developing type of person on Uranus, as the majority of this consciousness category has the opportunity to transfer to the more high-frequency and finely vibrating spiritual energies on other planets in the solar system, be it on Neptune where intuition and healing power belong, or on Venus where Crystal energy and love-intelligence belong.

∞ ∞ ∞ ∞ ∞ ∞ ∞ ∞ ∞

The energy on Uranus is thickly forested and often completely impassable and there is a wealth of natural creatures, dwarves, trolls, gnomes, elves, etc. These creatures live in harmony among themselves in exactly the same way as the developing Uranus people live in harmony with each other in places where the energy is less terrestrial and where there is no impassable forest growth. The reason for the harmony is that everyone lives more or less isolated and undisturbed on the terrestrial level on Uranus, while at the mental level they are closely intertwined and constantly challenge both themselves and one another.

In fact, all the rebellious Uranus people here on Earth represent the many trolls and other natural creatures that exist on Uranus. It is therefore no surprise at all that they don't like being controlled by other people or cooperating with them, as they are not human beings themselves!

The rainforest energy comes from Uranus and the fact is that the rainforest is, at some point, destined to disappear from the Earth's surface, in order that the remains of past highly-evolved societies, here on Earth, can be made visible to mankind.

The Uranus energy is thus the messenger of energy and knowledge from another era, which in this case, is far back in time as far as Earth is concerned but which is nevertheless still interesting and relevant for contemporary Earth people.

The old spirit knowledge from the very developed societies of the past will only come to the surface when enough people have connected directly to God's power on Earth, so that they are fully conscious of their dharma and personal life tasks in the Golden energy here on Earth.

NEPTUNE

Neptune is inhabited by angels on every level. Furthermore, the planet represents Jesus's energetic hinterland, where healing takes place and people intercede for themselves and others on the physical and spiritual level here on Earth.

However, the treatment of bodily imbalances using chiropractic, reflexology, acupressure, herbalism, etc. is controlled by Uranus, where most alternative practitioners here on Earth have their spiritual source.

In the human aura, as the energy moves up into the 5th dimension's Crystal energy and then into the 9th dimension's Crystal energy in the human aura and body, personal energy begins to relate to the Christ energy on Venus. As the energy moves up into the 13th dimension of the human aura, body and energy network, it relates to God's power on Earth.

Because of his spiritual hinterland on Neptune, we can consider Jesus as being an ancient archangel who, on a personal level, was willing to sacrifice himself and his life to spread the message of God's power to humanity here on Earth. God's power on Earth is in fact Christ's rightful spiritual home because of the very highest frequencies in his energy system. Also, he had, and still has, a direct spiritual connection to the Pleiades.

The many people on Earth who invoke the Jesus Christ energy in crisis situations when seeking help and assistance are thus invoking both the deeply healing Neptune energy and the purest form of the Venus love-intelligence at the same time. This is a very strong spiritual force where 'Jesus' represents the human aspect and 'Christ' represents the spiritual aspect.

The Christ-Venus energy, unlike the Jesus-Neptune energy, is very direct and does not relate to life through suffering. Christianity basically emerged as a form of religious cooperation between Neptune and Venus, where the Neptune energy gradually became less self-sacrificing in relation to other people as well as to the Whole. So even though the planet Neptune was first discovered here on Earth in 1846, Neptune energy has been present in human 'angelic form' since the birth of Jesus. He was the Neptune energy in a completely pure form, whose goal was to help humanity by taking on all their burdens.

∞ ∞ ∞ ∞ ∞ ∞ ∞ ∞ ∞

Since Neptune is home to the completely pure healing energy that comes directly from the heart, many of the planet's inhabitants have had no problem whatsoever with sacrificing themselves and suffering on the personal level in their many lives around the solar system. In reality, they have only been energetically preserved on their own home planet, as they have almost always chosen to sacrifice themselves on behalf of the Whole in every place they have stayed, hoping to be able to contribute to opening up the heart energy in their often unenlightened fellow human beings.

However, it is very rare that Neptune people on the everyday conscious level understand the energetic context behind their often very challenging lives on other planets, including here on Earth. Common to them all though is that their intuition and subconscious minds continually make them aware that there is not something wrong with them, no matter how much those around them are trying to convince them otherwise. They therefore believe that the development will probably turn to their advantage sometime in the future, as they would otherwise have given up on life a very long time ago.

Many of them often manage to pay the psychiatric system one or more visits during their lives here on Earth but still they have a very strong inner conviction that there is an overall meaning to everything in their lives; either that there is something more they need to learn, or else that they have to go through certain things in life, so that those around them can learn from these experiences.

In reality, it is totally impossible to smash the heart energy of Neptune people to smithereens no matter how hard life is, since, according to the Neptune energy, it is through the heart that the highest spiritual energy of all operates in we humans. It is easy to disturb their mental and psychological balance, so that outwardly they appear to be disturbed and confused when around other people. However, if they can surround themselves with stillness, they recover very quickly and can deal with almost any challenge that life may throw at them.

Neptune people would never ever be able to integrate Earth energy into their energy systems during their lives here on Earth if they did not go out and mingle with other different types of people. It is therefore paramount for all Neptune people to learn to function and hold their own energy in the terrestrial sphere. This is achieved partly by exposing themselves to energetic noise, which their neighbours on Uranus are especially good at without even being asked. Uranus people actually make a lot of noise, both when they are speaking and when they are thinking. Moreover, they are masters of telepathy, where they try to read those around them in order to influence them to do things in a certain way.

Uranus people also have the bad habit of often interfering in other people's energies, a bad habit which mostly affects Neptune people because they are able to pick up all energies and imbalances in their vicinity at a very finely vibrating and high-frequency spiritual level in their energy systems. So even though Uranus people primarily make a noise on the physical and terrestrial levels, Neptune people register all noise with 100% strength on the physical level, from where the noise spreads to their spiritual energy.

It is therefore no surprise that many Neptune people often hear voices from people who are not present and that they sometimes feel mentally disturbed because of the inability of those around them to keep their energy to themselves.

Neptune people have no Earth energy on their home planet and on a personal level, this creates some very basic existential problems for them here on Planet Earth especially if they have not been pressurised from birth to relate to and to integrate Earth energy in their lives and personalities. As a result, many of them, with or without reason, tend to believe that they have had a difficult childhood.

It is obviously a huge cultural shock for any little angel who comes to Earth from the high energy frequencies of Neptune to be born into some of the heaviest terrestrial material found here on the planet. It is fortunate that many Uranus and Pluto people are more than willing to accept these little angel-people with open arms on a soul level, as who would not want to have a baby with very high spiritual energy which can unconsciously be drawn upon when you are yourself lacking energy?

Neptune babies and children are quite outstanding for this purpose. The same is true for all Neptune adults who have not yet learned to set boundaries in relation to those around them. They can actually give all their energy and all their belongings away without getting anything in return and they even think they have done the right thing, even if afterwards they find themselves without a roof over their heads.

Neptune people are totally selfless and for that reason rarely have money and other material property. They will also give their last penny to help people in need, regardless of whether they know the people or not. If someone claims to have Neptune angel energy and has a lot of money in his/her bank account at the end of the month, it can be guaranteed that they don't have pure Neptune heart energy.

Many of the poor and unfortunate Americans that the television programme 'Extreme Makeover Home Edition' chooses to help by providing them with wildly lavish houses with room for lots of people are actually often Neptune people who have sacrificed everything they owned in order to help their children, family members and other people in need.

Regarding Neptune children, Uranus and Pluto people still like to receive Neptune babies into their earthly families with open arms, even though these children are now being born with a much more holistic consciousness and Crystal energy on every level.

∞ ∞ ∞ ∞ ∞ ∞ ∞ ∞ ∞

It has always been hugely important for all Neptune angels to be able to preserve as much of their original energy balance as possible in their many incarnations here on Earth. Otherwise, they would, as mentioned earlier, never get really grounded enough to be able to get the terrestrial substance properly integrated into their energy systems. It has therefore been necessary for them to ally themselves with some heavier and more primitive, physical, terrestrial energies, preferably some-one they know from their home planet. In this case, the choice has very naturally fallen on Uranus and Pluto, because these two planets, along with Neptune, are among the last to arrive in our solar system and therefore also on Earth.

On the soul level, this has unfortunately meant that Neptune people have easily let themselves be influenced psychologically and mentally to take inappropriate directions when the two other planetary energies (Uranus and Pluto) have shown their worst sides. Neptune angels have therefore often lost their radiance, as well as their light and power, when they have been with pure Uranus or Pluto people.

Today this cannot happen, as the Crystal energy is present from birth in all Neptune children's auras and bodies as well as in their network structures. This means that Neptune people no longer have a feeling of being trapped in their own bodies, enclosed by exogenous heavy energies.

Neptune people have so far been the only ones in the solar system who have been able to incarnate outside it for a long period of time in order to get updated and upgraded on the consciousness level. Many Neptune people therefore have a very strong relation on the consciousness level to the Pleiades, as well as to Sirius A and Orion.

The Pleiades are home to a very homogeneous and extremely high-frequency spiritual angel and balance energy, consisting of seven stars and seven development stages. In a very short space of time, Neptune people can thus have cosmic insight and balance integrated into their consciousness systems, similar to the energy that originally existed in the first seven planets in our solar system on the soul level. On the Pleiades though, the energy is integrated on the spirit level, which is a huge advantage for any Neptune people who want to take part in the development of the Golden energy here on Earth.

Sirius A is home to a very strong, laser-like, mentally focused intelligence, which was previously used to help certain chosen Neptune people to transform their thoughts so that they could take some far more constructive paths. However, this task of helping is currently being carried out by Venus.

∞ ∞ ∞ ∞ ∞ ∞ ∞ ∞ ∞

As mentioned earlier, Neptune first entered into our solar system on the visible level of integration from about 1846, when the planet was discovered by means of calculation and observation. From an energy and climatic aspect, Neptune is a temperate planet with a tendency towards cold and frost the further one moves up in frequency. The Water element is strongly represented here, both in liquid and in frozen form. All the animals we know from the polar regions of Earth, such as polar bears, seals and penguins, originally come from Neptune.

PLUTO

Pluto is an extremely small and overpopulated planet which is, from a purely astronomical point of view, not a planet per se but a dwarf planet.

Most people on Pluto are of the conviction that the more people there are who share the same opinion, the better it is. Consequently, the concepts of mass consciousness and majority come from here and it is generally very easy for power-hungry and energetically strong people to exercise power on Pluto. Pluto people are like flock animals who are extremely submissive and obedient to the authority of those who have had the courage to stand up and fight for a particular cause, especially if they were authentic front-line fighters who end up surviving the battle without being killed.

On Pluto, if a front-line fighter dies in the heat of battle, he usually ends up becoming a martyr who will be praised after death for his extraordinary efforts.

However, if a front-line fighter wins the battle, he or she can very easily turn into a dictator who believes that they are allowed to do anything in the surrounding world without having to excuse their bad deeds.

It is therefore not surprising that, for example, a certain kind of Islam is practised by a number of Pluto people on Earth, even though Islam originates from Jupiter in a very pure and lofty spiritual form similar to Buddhism. Religious fundamentalism has its roots on Pluto as when Pluto energy descends, it often tries to exclude anyone who does not fully support the community's views.

Pluto people generally believe that if just one person with a strong belief is able to integrate great spirituality into their energy systems, this spirituality will automatically rub off on all the other people around them, if the person is strong enough in his faith. This is how the energy affects the human masses on Pluto but it works in a different way here on Earth if you have another planetary background. For example, Muslim Jupiter people do not live from a belief that the more places their religion is represented around the Earth, the faster it will become a world religion. Pluto people, however, do.

Unlike several of the other planets in the solar system, they did not know about spiritual energy on Pluto before they became a part of the integration process in the solar system. This happened around 1930, when Pluto was discovered by an amateur astronomer on Earth. They have instead practised higher consciousness in a physical form, where people have been assessed on their actions.

In our solar system, the Yin-Yang symbol is often connected with Pluto, where the concepts of light and dark operate as two separate units, which together, must try to find a balance in the individual. It is therefore perfectly acceptable, for example, to behave badly one day, provided you remember to repent of your actions and to ask forgiveness the next day. This is reflected in the Catholic Church, where confession followed by absolution has always served as an offsetting factor for those who have sinned.

Catholicism is basically a Neptune-Mars-inspired religion, where Pluto later replaced the Mars energy.

Financial criminality, fraud and abuse, where attempts are made to survive from day to day, have their origins on Mars. However, the Mafia, in the form of organised economic criminality with a wealthy and power-hungry leader at the top and a hierarchical structure with a lot of petty gangsters at the bottom, has its source on Pluto because of the religious approach to life and the mix of the hunger for power and the flock mentality that is found there. Pluto energy is most visible in the Italian Mafia that has spread to the USA, among other places. However, Mafia-type organisations with a mixture of Pluto and Uranus energy can be found in regions such as Russia, China, South-east Asia and South America, where behaviour can be especially brutal and war-like.

∞ ∞ ∞ ∞ ∞ ∞ ∞ ∞ ∞

On Pluto, faith and collective consciousness are regarded as being superior to anything else – superior even to humanity – which means that they have a rather cavalier attitude towards human life. People are thus sacrificed for the powers that be, as the belief is that new children can always be brought into the world should the need arise.

Mass consciousness plays a part in people's attitudes to life in the Pluto energy and any lifestyle choice that is not mainstream will have no place on Pluto. Children somehow do not belong to their own parents. Instead, they belong to the family and the clan or the overall authority. This is harsh for anyone whose thinking is based on the importance of the individual and who may get trapped around their children because they have married into Pluto-controlled family systems.

The cult of beauty also comes from Pluto, where there are a lot of very beautiful people due to the great focus on external values. On an unconscious level, however, they cultivate all sorts of monsters and anxiety-inducing elements, which is why having nightmares comes from here. There is also tremendous focus on producing and trading beauty remedies as well as euphoria-inducing and sedative drugs, such as opium. These are used to deaden the underlying fear in the population.

However, the euphoria-inducing drugs which thrive all around the planet today and which make people 'hyper' and ecstatic come primarily from Uranus.

If Pluto people don't get what they want in their relationships, they can often use silence and psychological terror to manipulate their partners and their children. Ultimately, they have no inhibitions about using violence to achieve their goals but in general they can easily control their aggression so that it is expressed in a more appropriate manner. Pluto people have the same extremely violent intensity and destructive force in them as a nuclear bomb, which is why nuclear power belongs in the Pluto framework.

Those Pluto people who want to do something extra with their lives usually maintain an accelerated pace of day to day life, on both the human and energy levels, which is why those around them will choose not to follow them and/or try to compete with them. They also have an amazing ability to draw large amounts of energy out of the mass consciousness and for their own advantage, by creating extra attention and drama around themselves.

Many people out and about in the world still do not make use of their full consciousness, which is why very conscious Pluto people often find it perfectly normal to borrow some of this unused consciousness energy in order to become more successful in their physical lives.

Ethics is, unfortunately, not Pluto people's strong point, therefore they can greatly benefit from associating with spiritually aware Jupiter and Venus people who do not allow themselves to be controlled by Pluto' outwardly-focused energy. Moreover,

Neptune people can influence Plutonians to become more compassionate on the physical level, so they donate money to help people and regions in need if they don't want to contribute with physical assistance. Charities and large organised collections of money to help selected people, groups and places thus belong to the Pluto framework.

INFLUENTIAL PLANETS
OUTSIDE OUR SOLAR SYSTEM

The Pleiades, Sirius, Andromeda and Orion belong to the star systems outside our own which, throughout the ages, have contributed to and most influenced the overall consciousness development of our solar system. Here on Earth, these star systems attracted particular attention in prehistoric times when Earth's population was on the soul level. Nowadays, all children born on Planet Earth exist on the spirit level, where they are in daily contact with the spiritual consciousness in their bodies. They are therefore not so easily influenced by exogenous spiritual impulses that are not fully synchronised with Earth's newly activated Golden energy.

The star systems mentioned earlier have contributed each in their own way to strengthening interest in spirituality and magic, as well as the development of healing, love-intelligence and the use of cosmic mental intelligence and attraction here on Earth.

As already stated, none of the star systems have had a direct influence on the overall development here on the planet in recent times. However, information about them can and has been found during discoveries, such as artefacts, from earlier societies where numerous individual stars from certain star systems were worshipped as gods.

The four star systems have always operated on a more diffuse level behind the scenes in the spiritual hinterlands of both Uranus and Neptune, even though these two planets were only 'discovered' by modern astronomers in recent times. For the same reason, Uranus and Neptune were not officially recognised as being a part of our solar system until recently but that does not mean that they did not exist earlier or had not had an important role in the development of consciousness in our solar system and on Earth.

Both Uranus and Neptune were strongly represented on Atlantis, which was their ultimate attempt at cooperating on the spiritual-material level before they became a fully integrated part of our solar system. However, this cooperation process was not a success. At that point, about 13,000 years ago, both Uranus and Neptune were already in direct contact with the four star systems on the spiritual and mental levels. It was therefore not always easy for the seven original planets in the solar system to know whether it was pure Uranus and Neptune energies or other cosmic impulses that were coming to Earth via these two planets. This was simply because they were so new to the planetary cooperation and therefore an 'unknown quantity'.

The seven original planets – the Sun, the Moon, Mercury, Venus, Mars, Jupiter and Saturn – were the originators of the soul cooperation in our solar system back in time. This cooperation was based on the system of developing consciousness that they already knew about from Orion's Belt, as the Orion energy had had responsibility for cosmic destiny. At that time, the Orion consciousness development system was supposed to teach everything that existed all over the Cosmos to be in a state of constant process and to face truth and pain in order to be able to continually move forward in personal consciousness development. The Moon was designated as being primarily responsible for the soul reincarnation system and 'local' destiny.

In this highly structured system of soul consciousness development, there was no room to move as far outside the existing framework as both Uranus and Neptune did (and always have done) on the consciousness level. The seven old soul planets have therefore never quite been able to reconcile themselves with these two newcomer planets and their way of being and living. This resulted in numerous witch burnings and human sacrifices in ancient times of those people who came from these two planets before they were discovered by modern astronomers and gained an official place in the solar system.

Uranus and Neptune were primarily accepted as partners in the cooperation in the solar system because they are located on a frequency level in the same energy belt as the seven soul planets – just much farther from the Sun than the other planets. They were therefore accepted as part of the group and it was also agreed that they were welcome to contribute to the community with their respective consciousness strengths.

Pluto joined later, and maybe the future will bring even more planets, dwarf planets and moons which will fit into the community on the consciousness level.

THE PLEIADES

The Pleiades group of stars is known as the Seven Stars, the Seven Sisters and the Seven Divine Virgins.

It is a star cluster consisting of a collection of warm, blue, bright shining stars and contains a total of more than 500 young stars. The weak reflection nebula that surrounds the brightest stars is not directly related to the Pleiades. It is just a passing cloud of cosmic dust.

Alcyone, which is the Sun for the Pleiades, is the home of all the huge individualised angels who are responsible for balancing entire universes, galaxies and solar systems out in the Cosmos.

Pleiadian people are highly evolved spiritual beings who are at seven different levels of consciousness which correspond to the seven bright stars in the cluster. All of them support and assist the entire Cosmos, including humanity, here on Planet Earth, in its spiritual development.

The Pleiadian angels are those that come closest to the definition of positive, happy, indulgent, helpful and balancing angels, the kind that most people here on Earth associate with 'true' guardian angels.

All Pleiadian angels who are born into a human body are considered to be real 'star seeds', stardust and star suns, who have come here to bring light, ease and cosmic knowledge to Earth and to humanity. In other words, they are regarded as angels of God that have a direct lifeline to God and to the Holy Spirit. Consequently, most people in their vicinity have a natural expectation that these angels will always help humans, animals and Earth to achieve balance.

Pleiadian energy represents high-frequency sound, vibration and balance on the subtle and cosmic levels and most singers with divinely beautiful singing voices come from the Pleiades. The seven basic colours of the rainbow also come from the Pleiades and relate to the energy of each of the seven clear, luminous stars. Rainbow people, and also people with rainbow-coloured energy in their auras, are Pleiadian people who have completed the seven steps of overall consciousness development that God's angels can go through on the Pleiades.

Most Pleiadian angels normally specialise in radiating energy and healing, which they do with the help of one or two of the seven basic energies when they are on assignment in the Cosmos. Consequently, there are few Pleiadian people here on Earth who actually have rainbow energy in their auras, because it would then give their dharma a very broad spectrum. It is also worth noting that the rainbow energy in their auras will always appear along with the type of aura with which they are born here on Earth. This means that Pleiadian people born on the soul level may well have rainbow energy in their auras but unfortunately they will only be able to radiate a very small part of their great divine consciousness potential. This is because the soul aura has certain radiance constraints compared with the Indigo and Crystal auras.

For example, if Crystal children are born with rainbow energy in their auras, then the rainbow energy will, where necessary, amplify their Crystal energy and make the aura shine extra powerfully because both the Pleiadian and Venus energies contain Crystal energy – although in two very different ways. The Pleiadian Crystal energy is much less terrestrial and condensed in its structure than the Venus Crystal energy.

Pleiadian people are always spreading loving and uplifting messages whether they circulate in large or small groups, where they often have almost identical energies, or whether they are all alone and strong in expressing their personal consciousness. Wherever they are, they always surround themselves with balance and are very positive in everything they do.

They are always connected to the divine impulse and the divine flame deep within instead of identifying with God outside of themselves. Furthermore, they have the same overall divine intention in life, no matter what their level of consciousness may be. If they need to succeed in a particular matter, they are able to connect in a problem-free and very natural way with each other's energies without feeling resistance or competition. Everyone contributes to the community at all times in the best way they can, in order to succeed. This is a trend which we will be seeing more and more of, around the USA, from 2016 onwards.

Pleiadian people have an extremely strong and well-developed sense for and inner knowledge about everything. They also seem to know what is going to happen in the future. They have often had this innate insight all their lives. If they feel that those around them cannot relate to their natural way of communicating with God, they will often choose to slip into the background and become invisible to the people concerned, because they do not want to have to discuss or explain their divine approach to life and other people.

There are a great many positive things that can be said about Pleiadian people but to be succinct, their strengths lie primarily in the areas of education, communication, inspiration and propagation of balance in all contexts, be it on the physical, emotional, mental or spiritual level. Those around them are never in any doubt that they are receiving divine help directly from the highest source when they are being helped in life by a Pleiadian angel, whether it is in a professional or personal context.

Pleiadian people rarely appear naive in the same way that Neptune people do, simply because they believe so strongly that what they do, both for other people and for the Whole, is necessary, otherwise they would never do it. They will always follow the inner impulse deep within themselves and in their bodies. If it says "yes", they will choose to follow the impulse, because if they go against the truth in their own bodies, they will create personal bodily imbalance and will not be able to help anyone at all.

In April 2014, an opening was created for the Pleiadian energy to be able to access Earth directly. This opening will continue everywhere on Earth until the end of 2016, when many Pleiadian people will suddenly 'find themselves' and become visible to other people. The Pleiadian energy will be integrated into their bodies so that others will be able to clearly feel the divine impulse that is within these angels.

They will then finally be able to define themselves and their personalities from a consciousness and spiritual platform which will be accepted in the terrestrial sphere. Before this, they often had to make themselves invisible in order not to provoke all sorts of outwardly-focused and/or logically thinking people with their hidden consciousness resources that could not be explained in terrestrial terms. However, there are also many people who have wanted to take the credit for the positive energy and atmosphere which the Pleiadian angels have brought with them everywhere on Earth.

Interestingly enough, many Pleiadian people, because of the new collaboration with Earth, have been helped to learn to distinguish between who is worth helping and who to avoid. Due to their internal and external focus on cosmic balance, it appears that they are born masters in sorting and balancing energy between people and in their personal relationships This means that other people will no longer be able to latch on to their energy and radiance.

As a result, many people on Earth will then start clearly feeling their own energies and possible imbalances without being able to draw on other people's energy, balance and reserves. This will, in many cases, lead to them 'suddenly' feeling a great need to surround themselves with balanced Pleiadian people who can help them to attain balance and joy in their lives, bodies and minds. Pleiadian people will suddenly be respected and rewarded for this, without them in any way risking becoming big-headed or self-satisfied, just because there is a large and increasing interest in their personal energy and radiance.

SIRIUS

Astronomers on Earth have so far observed three stars in the constellation of Sirius, known as Sirius A, B and C. Sirius C was observed only a few times back in the 1920s/1930s. These three stars are only in contact with Earth because of their cooperation on the consciousness level with certain planets in our solar system.

Sirius A is twice as heavy as our Sun and it is 20-25 times more luminous than the Sun. This makes it the brightest and most luminous star in the night sky in Earth's northern hemisphere. The constellation of Sirius is constantly moving closer to our solar system, so at some point in the future, in many thousands of years, it will undoubtedly become a part of our solar system.

Sirius B is a white dwarf with a diameter almost equal to Earth's. It circles Sirius A in an ecliptic orbit that takes 50 Earth years and is a massive and very powerful star, given its small size. In those periods when Sirius A and B are closest to each other, violent magnetic discharges occur which affect our entire galaxy, solar system and Earth too. This happened most recently in 1949 and 1993.

Sirius C is a very small black dwarf which Sirius A and B both orbit but its existence has not yet been confirmed by modern scientists.

In spiritual and theosophical circles, Sirius A is referred to in several contexts as one of the greatest spiritual messengers of divine energy from the Central Sun of our solar system. The Central Sun is a higher consciousness source consisting of a male and a female God-vibration, which is responsible for coordinating the overall development of consciousness in several universes simultaneously. Many great beings of light and solar angels come from there.

When these great spiritual beings from the Central Sun are born as physical people here on Earth, they most frequently appear as highly spiritual people who have an extraordinarily well-developed spiritual consciousness as well as direct contact with alien universes and overall dimensions of consciousness in everyday life, whilst never losing their inner balance, bodily contact and grounding. Under normal circumstances, this is very difficult to achieve when an 'ordinary' human being has anything to do with extra-terrestrial states.

Sirius A is thus a propagator of energy from the Central Sun on a par with, amongst others, Venus and the Pleiades but it does not share, in an identical way, the Central Sun's comprehensive spiritual consciousness and cosmic insight. This means that not all Sirius A people have strong light energy in and around them even though Sirius A is an extremely luminous star. However, they often have a strong inner yearning on a consciousness level that makes them feel drawn to the light and out into the eternity of the Cosmos.

When they are reaching out into the Cosmos with their thoughts and terrestrial consciousness, they are connecting primarily with a mixture of strong mental space energy and universal love energy, which is the energy that they know from Sirius A. At this moment in time Sirius A energy can only be perceived, as far as most people are concerned, through the human brain and not with the consciousness of the terrestrial body. Consequently, the energy receives a very strong mental twist that makes many Sirius A people totally lose their sense of physical time and space if they begin to communicate on the consciousness level with cosmic creatures and energy states or connect with extreme forms of thought which belong outside Earth's energy field. Quite simply, they risk losing contact with their bodies and with the terrestrial dimension and in so doing, they completely lose their grounding.

Both Sirius A people and those with whom they surround themselves often experience dizziness if the Sirius A people are experiencing imbalance in the body, because they have too much light energy in their energy systems.

People with Sirius A energy are visionary and often have a well-developed mental intuition and clarity, combined with cosmic wisdom and insight. They are passionate about creating the same type of highly developed states, structures, thought forms and realms of consciousness here on Earth that they know from home.

Both Sirius A and B represent the Master Energy outside our solar system, whereas Venus represents the Master Energy within our solar system.

Sirius people are said to be the most talented architects in the Cosmos when it comes to the development and creation of structures and systems that can convey cosmic knowledge in an intelligent way. Sirius A takes care of all development and dissemination of light and spiritually-oriented energy, whereas Sirius B focuses on the darkness that can be equated with the condensed, material, form-creating energy that we know a great deal about on Planet Earth. Together, they are responsible for developing and maintaining the overall balance between mental intelligence and love-intelligence in the Cosmos.

Seen from a terrestrial perspective, Sirius A represents the creative mental energy which seeks the truth in amorphousness and then creates both a mental template and a mental expression based on its observations. This mental template can take many different forms; art, architecture, philosophy, mental development methods and learning tools, as well as new ways of living together, etc. which people here on Earth can use to expand their personal consciousnesses and thought universes.

Sirius B people are often perfectionists who are controlled by their own shadow side. This shadow side mostly causes them to express themselves in a very structured, controlling, finicky and sometimes power-hungry way. They show no willingness to compromise or to accommodate the needs of others.

Everything must be totally and utterly correct to the minutest detail and correspond to their personal inner vision and mental reality, which rarely matches the external reality and opportunities that exist here on Earth. Their satisfaction with their lives and the extent of their personal happiness are measured at all times by the extent to which it is possible for them to realise their inner vision in everyday life, both materially and emotionally - the mental part of their consciousness is always running in top gear.

Sirius C people always have an extremely strong need to live on the frontier of life and death, so they often challenge life and themselves to be constantly improving and excelling. Because of their physical-mental approach to life, they are constantly pushing their bodies to greater and greater achievements.

Sirius C is referred to as the Night Sun and people with a lot of Sirius C energy are capable of consciously becoming both alcoholics and drug addicts in order to taste life in all its aspects. They often have an unnatural thirst because there is a fierce fire burning in their materially condensed body energy, but not in their spirit. One can describe them as being like an oversized brain, where the actual body is a well-equipped turbo engine which needs to be kept running continuously. As a result, they are also very resourceful in terms of finding new activities and areas where they can go beyond their own previously-established boundaries.

Unfortunately, Sirius energies can often create major problems for people here on Planet Earth if they have no other planetary impulses with which to balance their personalities and Sirius-consciousness; Sirius energy in its pure form is very committed in all its undertakings and finds it difficult not to get involved more than 100%. Pure Sirius A and B people are extremely goal-oriented and don't normally relax until the goal has been reached, regardless of the personal human cost of success. Unfortunately, the goal is the most important thing for them and not the road they take to get there.

Personal stress and economic crisis are thus some of the very obvious consequences to which Sirius people expose both themselves and those around them in their terrestrial lives, as they do not like to compromise regarding their ideals. For the same reason, they also risk 'managing' to spend money they do not have in order to complete their idealistic projects.

Consequently, the Venus energy, which has been responsible for the development cooperation in our solar system regarding the entry of the Crystal energy on Earth from around 2000, was obliged to exclude the Sirius energy from this process, because the Sirius energy is far too extreme in many contexts and always prioritises the ends rather than the means. This means that, in many areas, the Sirius energy does not fully understand Earth's role in the overall development cooperation in the solar system. This is where attempts are being made to accommodate the development of as many different levels of consciousness and people as possible instead of only favouring the most able or the most high-frequency intelligent people.

Here on Planet Earth, the development of people in general is not assessed on the basis of their professional qualifications but rather on their potential consciousness and human qualifications. After all it is much easier to train and develop an able, positive-thinking person with their heart in the right place than it is to teach a professionally skilled and super-intelligent person to be a good, loving person. Being loving and personally accommodating is not necessarily very easy for most super-intelligent people. However, one of the major goals for the overall development of our solar system is to reconcile love and intelligence in the same expression of energy in everyone.

If the Sirius Energy had been at the negotiating table in the Crystal period, then Earth would never have had the chance, at the end of 2012 and following the demise of the soul energy, to be allowed, once again, to use its great power and strength to control all future development on this planet in a new and positively creative direction. The Sirius energy was, and remains, in favour of dichotomising the energies in the Cosmos and on Earth into light and dark, where light would have the upper hand and darkness would be broken down. Ultimately this would mean the demise of Earth, as if all dark and condensed material energy were to disappear from this planet, then not only Earth but all human and animal bodies would be broken down, dissolved and illuminated by light particles and the same would happen to nature. All material energy which has a physical form and a physical expression would be transformed into pure cosmic knowledge and intelligence without retaining its physical form; consequently much precious consciousness experience and insight, the creation of which has taken millions of years in our solar system, would go to waste.

Both Sirius A and B people are, however, slowly beginning to understand that they will not be able to have any influence over our solar system – and certainly not in the new creative Golden development flow that is in the process of being activated on Planet Earth – if they refuse to adapt to the current development opportunities and make the balance energy the ultimate goal in their lives. In the future, therefore, we will see more and more Sirius people gradually beginning to behave in a humane and compassionate manner in their relationships with other people. They will also begin to cooperate with other planetary types without trying to control their thoughts and push them in any particular direction.

ANDROMEDA

Andromeda is the largest neighbouring galaxy to the Milky Way, which is the galaxy of our solar system.

A galaxy is a vast collection of stars that are bound to one another by gravitational attraction. The Milky Way and Andromeda are both spiral galaxies, which as the name suggests, have a spiral structure and rotate around their own centres. Seen from Earth, the Andromeda galaxy is the biggest, brightest and most luminous of all the galaxies in the night sky.

The Andromeda galaxy is moving on a frontal course directly towards us here in the Milky Way, so in about four billion years, a fusion of the two galaxies will begin and it will end in approximately six billion years. The two galaxies will then collide and form a hybrid galaxy, which is a very large elliptical galaxy.

On the pure consciousness level, Andromeda energy represents the love-intelligence of the cosmic heart, which in the future will take over management of the entire Cosmos. There is a passion here to spread cosmic knowledge, insight and energy at a very high and often scientifically based level in a creative, abstract and sometimes boundless way. It is hoped that the Cosmos can be helped in the strengthening of the integration of all its different galaxies and universes, as well as that of all possible existing energy expressions.

Here on Earth, there are so far only very few spiritual people who can relate to consciousness at this scientifically focused, high-vibrating spiritual level, which may often seem to be very idealistic compared to the purely intuitive approach to spirituality that most spiritual people know today.

Andromeda is probably the star system which has taken on the biggest task in the Cosmos. Therefore, Andromeda people here on Planet Earth usually have many extra challenges in carrying out their dharma compared to other people. This is because their dharma often contains elements and components which are very spiritual and developmental on the consciousness level and it can be difficult to fit it into the often logically conditioned existing framework and environment in which the task belongs. This could be in the scientific, technological or artistic worlds where spirituality at a high-frequency cosmic level does not normally belong.

The Andromeda energy lies latent in the consciousness of many spiritual people with Sirius and Pleiadian energies but it will be many years before it has the opportunity of being expressed in a concrete and visible way in the terrestrial framework. This is due to the fact that before the Andromeda energy can penetrate down into the terrestrial material, in order to be expressed on a visible level in people's consciousnesses here on Earth, the Sirius energy must first find its way into the visible daily consciousness level of everyday life. The truth is that many more people on Earth can relate to the love-intelligent energy in the brain rather than in the heart, however strange that may sound.

ORION

Orion cooperates with Sirius A, amongst others, and has, for hundreds of thousands of years, helped to keep our solar system on a very slow rate of development by using the veil of illusion. This veil made everything look different from how it was in reality, with the aim of keeping humanity on the soul level with limited access to its own spiritual potential. With the demise of soul energy on Planet Earth, the veil can now be lifted so that people can actually begin to see one another as they really are.

The Orion energy has always looked on, saying nothing while things have been going the way they are intended in our solar system and here on Earth. It has never tried to interfere with destiny. There is no free will in the Orion Energy, which sometimes seems to be both under enchantment and mesmerised.

The energy merely watches and moves in a kind of parallel to Earth's energy universe and it is always in the midst of its own destiny and its own drama, without seeking answers as to why things are as they are and without searching for alternative development paths. In many ways, the Orion energy represents the stagnation of consciousness, where many of the same things occur over and over again. Consequently, there is no longer any room for this energy in our solar system – and certainly not on Earth – where clarity and the visible development of things is desired on both the material and the spiritual levels.

Since 2009, the people who have had this eternally repeating Orion tendency clearly represented in their personality have started, to an ever increasing extent, to be 'taken away' from Earth (they die), even though they may have been very successful in terms of their careers. The reason is that if they have not also been able to develop on the personal level, their career success alone will not suffice in Earth's energy on the Crystal level, as this requires responsible and conscious development in all areas of life.

PHYSICAL ENERGY IS IMPORTANT
FOR COOPERATION IN OUR SOLAR SYSTEM

One thing common to the ten planets in our solar system is their physical radiance energy. It is this physical radiation energy that created the basis for the energies of the various planets being able to meet and connect with each other here on Planet Earth.

However there is no terrestrial energy on the planets where there is high-frequency spirit energy, and vice versa, Jupiter being an exception. As a result, we human beings here on Earth have to circulate between certain planetary energy combinations to move up and down in frequency if we are trying to move our attention from a terrestrial to a spiritual state of consciousness and vice versa.

Fortunately, several of the solar system's planets already had various forms of transversal cooperation when Earth was designated as the common integration and development planet for the solar system, otherwise it would have been a total disaster trying to bring such diverse planetary energies together here on Earth. The result would have been that all the people with terrestrial and spiritual energy respectively, would have been completely alienated and invisible to one another; many people are still invisible to one another today, thousands of years after the planetary cooperation was launched on Planet Earth.

In fact, it is only here on Earth that it is possible, using consciousness, to move around on all three energy levels – the terrestrial level, the physical radiance level and the spiritual level – at the same time.

Uranus people can therefore choose between having either

Uranus or Neptune radiance, as well as mental and psychic balance in their lives when they are on the physical level with their consciousness awareness. However, only the Neptune energy is represented in the higher energy frequencies on the spirit level in the outer part of the solar system, which is why Uranus people have to use Neptune energy to increase their frequency and expand their consciousness.

Neptune people who find themselves on the physical or spirit levels have two options in the downward direction – namely, Uranus or Pluto energy – if they wish to become more grounded and integrate terrestrial energy into their consciousness systems. They often choose the same planetary energy as their grounding every time they are born on Planet Earth, based on what influences they have around them.

We can say that many very spiritually conscious people have far more energy choices when they need to have terrestrial energy integrated into their consciousness than people with very terrestrial energy do when they need to move up in frequency onto the spiritual plane.

The fact that there is any difference at all between terrestrial and physical energy may surprise some people but this can be explained in a very simple way. The physical energy here on Planet Earth represents the radiation that occurs when a person's spirit energy and their terrestrial energy, power and grounding are all connected.

On other planets with other energy constellations than that of Earth, physically radiating energy may well exist without the simultaneous presence of terrestrial energy and spirit energy.

Terrestrial energy is solely concerned with the body and basic needs, such as food, drink, sleep, sex and the need to make money and so on; needs that have to be met in order for it to be possible to survive in a body in the highly condensed energy sphere found on Earth.

Physical energy in particular is important for us, as human beings here on Earth, because it is the only way in which we can recognise one another. We will therefore primarily respond to one another's physical energy and radiance if we have nothing else in common. In this way, strongly terrestrial and highly spiritual people will always have an opportunity to be able to relate to other people through their radiance if they have no other way of being able to recognise one another.

People who have large amounts of terrestrial energy will always be best able to relate to other people through the external and visible criteria in life, whereas very spiritual people will always assess their fellow human beings by looking at their inner values. In the context of all cooperation on Earth between people of different planetary backgrounds, it is of the utmost importance that the cooperating partners have their radiating energy in place so that others can relate to them on the human, physical level.

If a person's radiance and soul aura starts disappearing or breaking up because of grief, stress, illness, accidents and the like, it is extremely important to get the aura structure assembled again on the spirit level so that it can be continually updated and upgraded. You can learn more about this in the videos on our AuraTransformation™ YouTube channel: **www.youtube.com/ SennovPartners**.

THE DEVELOPMENT OF CONSCIOUSNESS ON EARTH

Besides the basic cooperation between the planets in our solar system which takes place each day in people's lives on Planet Earth, there are several other energies, impulses and factors that, each in their own way, affect the mutual will to cooperate here on the planet.

On the soul level, for many hundreds of thousands of years we have been operating with the influx of seven energy rays to Earth, equivalent to seven different cosmic energy influxes. These seven energy rays were initially related to the first seven planets in the solar system – the Sun, the Moon, Mercury, Venus, Mars, Jupiter and Saturn – the equivalent of the soul energy and the old spirit world in our solar system although the seven energy rays originated from the Central Sun.

Later, an opening was created for the influx of energy from the outer spirit world, where Uranus, Neptune and Pluto on the 9th to 11th rays belong, after which the number of energy rays was increased to 13.

The 8th ray was then created as a comprehensive ray consisting of feminine energy responsible for the first seven rays and the old spirit world and soul energy, while the 12th ray, consisting of masculine energy, was created as an overall ray of the new spirit world and the 9th to 11th rays.

In many contexts, the 13th ray is considered to be identical to Earth's spiritual-material energy which the other rays will eventually become an integral part of but the 13th dimension also represents the energy of Earth, so in many ways, the number

13 is identical to Earth's energy.

You can read about the 13 dimensions in my book, "The Crystal Human and the Crystallization Process Part I".

In the outer spirit world, people have never really allied themselves with the soul energy in the same security-hungry way as the seven original soul planets did. Having to incarnate on Earth, where the soul energy controlled the spiritual and consciousness development of the people with a very firm hand, using the karma and reincarnation systems, felt like torture to many Uranus, Neptune and Pluto people. Seen through the eyes of the outer spirit world, the concept of karma was exclusively created by God's Power in order to be able to exercise control over the troops taking part in the integration process of the various planetary energies in our solar system.

Everything on Earth is a direct reflection of what exists on the different planets in our solar system. The composition here on Earth is entirely new and unique, however and has never before been attempted. There are so many different elements that have had to be integrated at the same time and in the same place.

A large number of these forms of energy have unfortunately proved to be completely useless and highly destructive for the collective development here on Planet Earth and in the solar system. Attempts have therefore been made to eliminate them from Earth's energy on both the physical and the consciousness levels. Some of these elimination projects are very difficult to put into practice, which is why it will still take many years before all the elimination processes have been completed.

The elimination projects are, however, continuously given very high priority in the context of personal and consciousness development both on Planet Earth and on other planets around the solar system but sometimes resistance rages violently against certain changes because the planets do not always agree with one another. This is similar to politics in the EU and the UN, where countries and energies which are very different from each other try to work together to create a balanced whole for the benefit of everyone.

If, for example, there is a reluctance to change a type of behaviour or a mind-set on one particular planet but the change is necessary for the overall integration process here on Earth, something tantamount to civil war will arise in the minds of the people who come from that particular planet. The opposing forces will be extremely agitated until they have taken sides at the personal level in favour of either their home planet or the solar system as a whole and therefore of Earth.

In the summer of 1987, the Indigo energy began to stir in Earth's collective consciousness. The Indigo energy was chosen to lead people from the soul energy into the spirit energy via a transformation bridge that everyone had to cross in order to switch from the one level of consciousness to the other; everyone has to make a conscious choice to be able to cross this bridge as the consciousness shift will not just happen all by itself. If the decision is not made in a person's lifetime these days, it will happen instead when they die and the consciousness shift will take place on the other side of the veil; next time they incarnate, they will have the spirit energy in both body and aura. This consciousness shift can also take place while you are still alive thanks to AuraTransformation™, which is a permanent upgrade of the aura from the soul level to the spirit level.

In 1987, the Indigo energy took on the role of the New Time energy, after the Uranus energy, which was the New Age planet at the soul level. Babies began being born with Indigo energy in their auras. They still had soul auras like their parents but they had greater power and a stronger will and desire to change things than their parents had ever had. As a result, they started to rebel in different ways against the established systems, whether it was at school or out in the community, because they quite simply did not fit into the boxes that had been created on the soul level. ADHD began to spread like wildfire among young people and suddenly there were also adults with Indigo energy in their energy systems, who were unable to control themselves and their own behaviour. As the years passed, children were born with diminishing amounts of soul energy in the aura and with increasing quantities of Indigo energy.

From 1995, all children were born with an Indigo aura and they were completely themselves and had no desire whatsoever to follow their parents' and society's instructions if the parents didn't have an Indigo aura like them. It became possible for adults to have an Indigo aura in 1996 when AuraTransformation™ came through to Earth channelled through me. In the beginning though, it was only possible for adults to get an Indigo aura that was 3 centimetres thick but it was far better and created the basis for a much larger consciousness expansion than if they had continued with a soul aura like most other adults.

Up until 1998, the Indigo aura for these particular adults began to expand all by itself, so their Indigo auras eventually grew to the same size as those of the Indigo children. As a result, there are no aura-transformed adults anywhere that today still have a 'small' Indigo aura.

Around 2000, the Crystal energy began to show in the auras of new-born children. Some children were born with a mixed aura consisting of both Indigo and Crystal energies and from 2004, all children were born with a pure Crystal aura. After this, it also became possible for adults to have a Crystal aura following an AuraTransformation™ and fortunately, those who already have an Indigo aura, following an AuraTransformation™, can automatically upgrade their own auras to Crystal energy when they are ready. This often happens when they begin to crystallise at the cellular level in their bodies in the same way as when they crystallise in their auras.

Children who are born with an Indigo aura can also upgrade to a Crystal aura, in the same way as adults do when they and those around them are ready. This often depends on their parents. However, both groups may well benefit from one or more balancings during the process.

In 2009, all children were born as Crystal individuals with a Crystal aura and with crystallised body energy, that is to say with Crystal energy integrated at the cellular level in the body. This meant that they had high-frequency, love-intelligent Venus energy integrated into both their bodies and their auras.

At the same time their parents' generation began to integrate Crystal energy in the body and to body-crystallise, whether they had been aura-transformed or not. This happened automatically in several cases if the person lived close to nature or lived very healthily and was extremely conscious of what they exposed their body to. If they trained hard and did a lot of sport, where they had to discipline their body energy significantly more to achieve peak performance, there was a very high probability that they would body-crystallise quickly. However, it could not happen in less time than it takes for an unborn Crystal child to crystallise in the embryonic stage during pregnancy, because the embryo's energy is fully protected from external energies. This is not the case for the energy of adults in everyday life, so body crystallisation naturally takes longer for adults.

From 2013, all children were born as Crystal children with a Crystal aura, crystallised body and crystallised network energy.

They are therefore very aware of who they associate with and the reasons for this. They are perfectly able to manage all of their own energy and to retain it in the body. This is possible because they are fully crystallised in their personal energy as well as the auric and network energy surrounding them. Right from the moment of birth, they are closely related to a group of people whom they have yet to meet in physical life but whom they know from other layers of consciousness in their consciousness development. They are therefore fully conscious that they are part of a spirit family that will always be with them both when alive here on Planet Earth and in other universes.

Because these children are born with Crystal energy fully integrated on all levels of their consciousness system, the Golden energy will be activated in their body almost as soon as they are born, if it had not already begun to stir during pregnancy. However, this depends very much on the frequency of the mother's body energy during pregnancy and how much it can expand to create appropriate space for the child's energy. If the mother's energy cannot maintain a high enough frequency during pregnancy, the child will usually not activate the Golden energy in the body until sometime after birth. This means, among other things, that the child will suddenly be awake much more than usual and no longer needs so much sleep unless it is experiencing an energy deficit.

The activation of the Golden energy will get these Crystal-Golden children to completely naturally become happy little sociable energy bombs with very strong personal willpower and dynamism. Fortunately, the Crystal energy will make them begin to live out their dharma and life purpose at a very early age. These children have many life tasks that will be spread over the course of their earthly lives.

In the coming years, all children will be born as Crystal-Golden children with a Crystal aura, crystallised body, crystallised network energy and with the Golden energy activated on the cellular level in the body. The only consciousness development which will take place in their personal energy is when their auras slowly begin to become both compressed and amplified as they learn the things they need to learn on the consciousness level in order to be able to carry out their adult dharma. If they have nothing else to learn in order to carry out these life tasks, other than what they can learn in school, their auras will already be entirely compressed from birth.

The compression of the aura therefore, depends solely on how much the children have left to learn on the consciousness level to realise their dharma. However, they will definitely not be bored during their lives, as there will be plenty of challenging balancing tasks to address everywhere on Earth, even for new-born children.

Later this century, the Diamond energy will arrive – this process will only take place in the body but it will be reflected out into the aura. This energy cannot be activated if you still have a soul aura, even though you may be fully crystallised on the spirit level in your body energy.

CRYSTAL ENERGY IS NECESSARY
FOR GOOD RESULTS

As you have probably already understood, the Crystal energy is a crucial vehicle for Earth's creative and creating Golden energy, enabling it to unfold in a vital and constructive way, now that it has finally come to the surface after having been hidden in Earth's interior for an eternity.

The Crystal energy represents love-intelligence and balance, as well as a focus on truth, purity, overview, aesthetics, beauty, speed of thought and action, structure, responsibility and last but not least, a focus on personal dharma.

The Golden energy represents the spiritual-material creation and creative power in the body, with a focus on activity and movement, whilst having a flair for seeing the developmental opportunities and potential in everything around. It is therefore vital that you have the Crystal energy in place in your conscious-ness before the activation of the Golden energy takes place in your body, otherwise it would be like running around like a headless chicken without being able to see which direction you need to take and why.

With its broad overview on the consciousness level, the Crystal energy helps you to express Earth's Golden energy in a respon-sible, lively and balanced way. Since it has also helped in the phasing out of the energies of both the Moon and Saturn in Earth's energy sphere and in people's consciousness, it is fully up to date on how today's spiritual people operate in compari-son to people on the soul level. They can therefore help the population of Planet Earth transition into the Golden Age in a more balanced way than is possible for any of the other planets in the solar system.

The Crystal energy can easily help you to manage and balance your inner contradictions, when you are on the spirit level with your personal energy. It can even handle and balance other people's imbalances and contradictions too. This is partly done by you and the other people entering into clear agreements and defining the overall, crystal-clear guidelines for what you each expect from your fellowship and cooperation with one another.

The Crystal energy makes it very easy for you to plan and cooperate with others if you are on the spirit level with your personal energy and have a Crystal aura. You will then be able to benefit from all the preferred qualities of the Crystal energy in your everyday life, whereas you will need advice from people with Crystal energy if you still have a soul aura. Associating with Crystal children can help you to upgrade your body energy to the Crystal level if, for example, you work with children on a daily basis. However, your aura cannot be upgraded by itself from the soul level to the spirit level but your body energy and your way of thinking can.

The Crystal energy will help you to maintain a constant balance in all contexts and it has a focus both on you as an individual as well as on the various things that you are a part of in your life: family, friends, sports teams, the workplace, the community, your country, Planet Earth, the solar system, the universe or the Cosmos.

Furthermore, the Crystal energy will help you to remain balanced in relation to the Golden energy that exists in all people on Earth to a greater or lesser extent for the simple reason that they live on Earth. All of us have access to a certain amount of the creative force within us to use in different ways, depending on whether we are on the soul level or the spirit level with our personal energies. You will have the opportunity to read more about this later in the book.

To conclude my review of the planets in our solar system, I will, in the next chapter, look at Earth's Golden creation and creative energy and how it will affect everyone on Earth in the future, depending on where they are in life on the consciousness level. Later in the book, there are a host of other energetic explanations of what is happening on Earth in the Golden Age that began on 21 December 2012 and information about what you can do to get the most out of your life for the benefit of yourself and everyone and everything around you, in this spiritual-material creative energy.

THE GOLDEN ENERGY

The Golden energy is Earth's spiritual-material creation and creative force. The purpose of activating the Golden energy in the body is that it allows you to start putting your dharma and your life purpose(s) into practice in your life.

It is important that you do not share your dharma with other people. You may tell other people about your life visions but you should not get them to do things for you that you are predestined to do yourself. This would not benefit you or the other people concerned, because nobody on this Earth can succeed optimally with anything that is not a part of their personal life purpose.

It is therefore extremely important for everyone to have good contact with their own bodies in the Golden Age, as it is here that the dharma and life tasks of us humans are stored. If a 'wrong' body tries to succeed with a project that is borrowed or stolen from someone else, the project will be doomed to failure.

If you have Golden energy activated on the Crystal level in the body and you are involved with or try to exchange energy with people whose body energy is not on the Crystal level and who do not understand and respect your person or dharma, you risk having them trying to control you and the way you live your live.

Always remember, therefore, to keep your Golden energy and your creativity, as well as your creation and creative power, in your own body and take the energy with you wherever you go, in exactly the same way as you always take your body with you. That way, you will be the boss of your own life and in your own body and no one else will be able to have control over you or your materialisation power. Instead, they may experience the joy of being with you, where you are in personal balance and feel comfortable in your own body and therefore are able to inspire those around you. It is always entertaining to be in the company of people who have the Golden energy activated on the Crystal level in the body.

This is the way we, as people of the New Time, are expected to live in the Golden Age which began on 21 December 2012. It is now paramount to live a balanced life with a focus on ourselves as individuals and on everything around us. When we live like this, we can inspire those around us to live a life of balance with themselves and with others; this ideal way of life sounds simple on the surface, but it is still not an easy way to live for the majority of people here on Earth.

The Golden energy is your own unique body and materialisation energy. The energy only works in a balanced manner in the parts of the body that are already crystallised.

The more balanced and grounded you are in your body energy, the easier it will be for you to materialise and realise your ideas and visions on the physical level of life.

∞ ∞ ∞ ∞ ∞ ∞ ∞ ∞ ∞

As I stated earlier, it is impossible to copy or take other people's Golden energy into your body and energy field, because then you will not be able to succeed in whatever you wish to undertake. People can only succeed with their own personal version of the Golden energy; they will fail if they try to run on other people's life energy as other people's energy will not give life to their body in the way that their body needs it. This is due to the unique nature of each person's energy.

The pure Golden energy is very physically focused and contributes, with its incessantly initiative-taking impulse, to the creation of objects and conditions that make areas of daily life easier. The Golden energy can be an inventor, creative sex partner, games organiser for children, party planner and eternal optimist, always inspiring others.

The energy can sometimes come across as being overwhelming, for both themselves and others, if the Crystal energy, with its focus on dharma and the constructive and responsible use of energy, is not yet integrated in your body. In fact, the Golden energy can seem almost manic and uncontrollable at times, if it is not under control and in balance. It is thus a combination of the Crystal energy and the Golden energy that will be managing the lives of us humans for many years to come.

A universe deep within Earth's interior is in the process of being opened up, one which corresponds to the universe that we humans have contained in our physical cells. Deep in the interior of Planet Earth, the Golden energy of all mankind lies waiting for each individual person to be ready to activate his/her personal Golden energy. For those who do not have access to the Golden life-impulse in their bodies, there is no Golden energy in Earth's interior. This means that they are most likely not going to live long in the Golden Age where the joy of living is the No. 1 elixir of life which contributes to maintaining life in us humans for longer than average.

Earth's inner universe equates to the outermost region of the heavens, which corresponds to that which is undivided and to the essence of God; it doesn't equate in any way to the collective consciousness and the radiance that surrounds the Earth. So what many believe to be Earth's aura is rather the sum of all the auras and personal energy of humanity.

Earth has not yet opened up its internal creative potential and it will take thousands of years to open up this great force. Consequently, there are very few people today who are in full contact with the Golden Earth force in their body energy on the everyday consciousness level, even though they have great sensitivity towards their body and are well grounded.

Up until now, the Golden energy has only had the opportunity to express itself with great force through nature and animals but now it has become the turn of us humans to integrate and activate the energy – an energy which can be very difficult to master if you do not already have the high-frequency love-intelligent Crystal energy integrated into your body.

In this phase of Earth's evolution, the overall energy, with the assistance of the Crystal energy, has fortunately come so far that Earth's Golden energy cannot just flow freely into someone's energy and take control of their bodies and brains. There is therefore no risk that the reptilian brain and certain individuals' extreme, ungrounded ideas will take control of Earth due to people having been 'injected' with a force that they are unable to handle in a balanced way. It may not always look like that when you look around the planet but it really is so.

The focus of the Crystal energy on responsibility and balance ensures that at any given time the Golden energy will only gain access to people's bodies when they have clearly demonstrated to themselves and others that they can balance on a high-frequency level within themselves and in their everyday lives. The Golden energy will not, therefore become available to everyone, even though it is in the Earth beneath our feet.

Everyone is here on Planet Earth to raise the frequency of their own personal energy. Earth's energy and power do not need an increase in frequency and therefore Earth will never give her power away to anyone who cannot handle it. On the other hand, many people will get one, or more, chances in life to show what they can do and how far they can go on the consciousness level, if they have shown that they have great willingness to take on greater responsibility in their lives. If it turns out that they cannot maintain the high-frequency level that is expected without losing their personal balance, these opportunities and the Golden energy itself will be shut down again.

In people who are on the soul level and still have a soul aura, the Golden materialisation energy will often be expressed in a selfish, hyper and uncontrolled manner. This can be seen especially clearly in people who are not crystallised in the body or aura via an AuraTransformation™. They think they can do everything and are much wiser and more spiritual than everyone else. It is therefore obvious that the type of Golden energy that soul people have activated is not high-frequency Golden energy.

People at a soul level who have the Golden energy activated without being crystallised in the body usually do a lot for other people but unfortunately there are often personal and/or selfish motivations behind everything they do, even when doing good for others. They often seem downright disturbing to those around them with their forceful energy, because there is always activity in their energy, especially in the body. Their physical needs and bodily desires take up too much space in their own lives and the lives of other people.

The Crystal basis for the Golden energy being integrated into our bodies at a high-frequency level means that there will be a simultaneous focus on both individuality and the Whole. Golden energy entering the body does not therefore result in the Golden energy in a pure form, rather it is a Crystal-Golden energy which inhabits just the physical body and the aura stays as it is.

Humans can either have a soul aura, which keeps many adults stuck in the tracks through life that they are born into on the soul level, where life is governed by karma, or they can have an Indigo and/or Crystal aura, both of which belong on the spirit level. All children have been born on this level since 1995 with dharma and the free will to carry out their individual life purposes as suits them best.

The adults who have soul auras were all born into a personal life maze on the physical level, from which they can only escape when they eventually find the exit. For most people this doesn't happen until they are approaching the end of their lives, or when they reach a point where they have done all that they are predestined to do in life.

However, there is a large group of adults who are very conscious about updating themselves on the energy level and who therefore no longer have a soul aura. Many of these have had their aura upgraded through having an AuraTransformation™ to either an Indigo aura or a Crystal aura, which all children are born with today, or possibly through other consciousness transformation methods with which I am not acquainted.

∞ ∞ ∞ ∞ ∞ ∞ ∞ ∞ ∞

Earth has its own methods and it often leaves it to life to teach people the things that they need to learn. However, this by no means excludes the need to study or to learn by listening to others. So when the Crystal energy, with its focus on responsibility and love-intelligence, is integrated into a person's body consciousness, it is primarily the 'school of life' with all its high and low-frequency energies that, in the Golden Age, will be managing what people have the opportunity to learn on the consciousness level.

When we seriously begin making use of Earth's materialisation power, where we focus on succeeding in certain areas, we will often get our wishes fulfilled in both positive and negative ways.

Earth energy is in fact filled with contradictions and if you follow every contradiction to its completion, you will see that all energies are connected in different ways. The Golden energy is also filled with contradictions and the energy of duality, which is why, for example, it is possible to be closely linked to someone and also to set them free.

The goal-oriented Crystal energy, with its focus on balance and the Whole, makes it possible to establish 'crystal-clear' agreements and rules for what is expected of people in their lives and the progress of evolution here on Earth. The Crystal energy simply burns a path to the goal.

The Golden energy makes us committed, entertaining, productive, creative and happy with life and spreads a lot of joy when it feels inspired. It is therefore able to motivate those around it to make a huge positive difference in different contexts.

In the Golden Age, we are suddenly noticing every aspect all at once, where previously we might only have noticed either the physical or the spiritual side of things. So now we see everything we like as well as everything we do not like. This applies to everyone – even those who have not had their aura upgraded to Crystal level with the help of an AuraTransformation™.

In the future, this will be the primary reason why many people will choose to have an AuraTransformation™. They will need a much stronger, permanent protection and magnetism in their auras which can help them to keep alien energies out of their bodies and energy fields. It can be extremely difficult and time-consuming to have to manage your energy every day if you still have a soul aura.

On the Crystal level, everything is about balance, and in the Golden energy, it is an eye for an eye and a tooth for a tooth, which may be said to be a slightly different kind of balance. In the future, we will thus experience a mix of these two different types of balance, which will certainly be both exciting and challenging. However, one thing is certain and that is that Golden action without Crystal intelligence can in many ways be compared to a man without a brain.

IT IS IMPORTANT
TO SUPPORT THE RIGHT PEOPLE

Earth's energy is extremely observant regarding everything that happens on the planet and it continuously mirrors and reflects all our choices in life by creating an imprint of all our impulses, thoughts, feelings, actions, etc. These are stored in Earth's matrix and internal structure, which means that the imprints are not always visible on the surface of Planet Earth, so you can, for example, feel them in the air.

Just as our auras are able to radiate who we are, so that other people can get a sense of our personality before they have even met us or talked to us, so are similar impulses stored in the body. It is these impulses that are transmitted directly to Earth's interior due to the similarity of frequency between human and animal bodies and everything in nature and in Earth's energy structure itself.

It is therefore strongly advisable that everyone should support only those who are well-intentioned, as every time you support a person who behaves badly or has bad intentions, you risk delaying your own spiritual growth and personal development.

By supporting people who steal, cheat, lie or harm others, it will become visible to everyone that you are not yet able to make the right choices in life. But who knows? Maybe you have made the right choice by being with those people, as if you feel comfortable in their company, it must mean that you belong there with your current energy frequency, so there is perhaps no reason to change anything.

Choosing the 'wrong' people may also be due to you being very naive and unconscious about your own behaviour.

The result of inviting the 'wrong' people into your life is often that a lot of doors will close for you in the community, because you will be judged on your personal choices. Even more doors will be closed on the consciousness level, which is invisible to most humans. As a result, those who support negative and criminal people are not always very successful in life, or things often go wrong for them when they surround themselves with people who have low frequency and/or negative energies. Earth's power only supports unconscious and ignorant people to a certain point on the development front. So if they are to have any hope of getting more help from Earth's overall power, they need to expand their consciousness in one way or another in order to show that they are on the right path.

This means that every good deed done by unconscious or 'ignorant' people is in fact rewarded with extra help on the invisible level from Earth's inner power centre to motivate them to carry on in this vein, even if their intentions are not always the best.

If people are conscious of their bad choices in life, there will be no assistance from anywhere if they do nothing to change the situation for the better. So if they don't try to change things in a positive direction and if they continue to frequent those people and places where the bad things are happening, they are supporting the bad people and the bad energy with their own personal energy and this will stymie their personal development possibilities

It is therefore very important that you support the right people in life and that you avoid the wrong people or set limits on how much influence you allow them to have on your life. This does not mean that you cannot greet these particular people when you meet them on the street, but do not give them energy by talking a lot with them and about them or by supporting their projects.

If you have mistakenly sent too much energy in their direction, I strongly recommend that you use the energy exercises described in the two energy guides written by my husband and me, "The Little Energy Guide 1" and "Get Your Power Back Now!" This will help you to restore your personal and energetic balance. You can also take our online course on energy management that you will find links to on **www.annisennov.com** and **www. fourelementprofile.eu**.

YOUR PERSONAL BALANCE IS VITAL TO YOUR DHARMA

Many people find the developmental opportunities that are hidden in the Golden energy extremely interesting. It is important though to *always* keep your focus on maintaining the balance between the Crystal energy and the Golden energy to make sure you are also maintaining the balance between your dharma (life task) and your personal energy.

It is the balance between dharma and personal energy that is the most important thing in life, especially in the Golden Age; if you do not take care of yourself and take responsibility for having a personal balance in your life, it will become very difficult for you to successfully live your dharma.

Your personal balance and your dharma are specifically linked and it is your personal task to ensure that there is balance between these two major elements in life.

When you have activated the Golden energy in your body, it is your own energy that is activated. You will not receive a transfer or activation of any blueprint or power from the outside which will make you stronger and more creative and materialising than you already are.

You can be motivated and inspired by being with other people, and the more of you who motivate and inspire one another, the more you will stay motivated and inspired. It is important to keep the energy going in your own body and in your energy system and your everyday life so that you can begin to live your dharma (life purpose).

Your dharma will always be inspiring and appealing to you,

even if you sometimes have to fight for your cause. No one with Crystal-Golden energy in their energy systems has chosen easy life tasks in the lottery of life. We humans have to use our own Golden creation energy to pave a way forward which has often not been travelled by other people before us in the way that we may choose to do it.

Everything that has anything to do with the Golden energy is in some way new each time, because no two people and situations are ever alike and the Golden energy belongs exclusively in the body. Consequently, the way we express ourselves in our behaviour and through our bodies is essential for the manner in which we are successful and for the extent to which we are successful in creating a way forward in life that supports the fulfilment of our dharma. In the Golden energy everything is always expressed in a very individual way and it is seldom a repetition of what others have already done before

Mankind's deepest joy in life here on Earth, is linked quite simply, to us having the opportunity to live out the things in life that we are predestined to do, namely our dharma. Consequently, many people do not feel that they have a joyful life if they are not able do what they have been born to do. This applies regardless of whether they have the world's loveliest partner, children and friends, or not.

All people of all ages with a focus on the New Time have been born to achieve their personal life task(s) and their dharma and when they do that, the Golden energy automatically begins to stir in the body in cooperation with the Crystal energy and it becomes impossible to copy others or to try to be like them and no one will be able to succeed in doing anything that is basically not right for them personally.

The Golden energy contains the four elements of fire, water, earth and air as does the Crystal energy. Both energies also include the masculine and feminine energies and when all these elements are in balance with one another in our energy system and we dare to be ourselves, our personal wheel of life begins to roll all by itself. It is this wheel of life and the collaboration between the Crystal and Golden energies (responsibility, combined with creativity) that enable us to contact our dharma in our bodies. When we become one with our dharma, we know that we are truly living a meaningful life.

MATERIAL ENERGY CAN ALSO BE PURE

In the spiritual-material Golden energy here on Planet Earth, everything has structure. Only pure spirit has no structure, system, form, subdivision and matrix because pure spirit is a pure state of being.

The more material and condensed an energy is, the more structure it has and the more immaterial and spiritual an energy is, the less structure, system, form, subdivision and matrix it has.

For us humans here on Earth, it is important to be as pure and simple as possible in our matrix and structure all the way back to our spiritual source (the source we originate from), as then all energies, systems and personal qualities that are built on top of our pure spiritual source will be correspondingly pure.

If we don't become completely pure in our energy all the way back to that seed from which our spirit and our life impulse stem, different kinds of problems will emerge later in the spiritual-material energy sphere of our lives. It could be in connection with our health, our economy, our physical environment, our human relations or other things, since the lack of purity in the spiritually condensed energy layers in our body will get our body and our surroundings to respond in an unbalanced way.

So the purer we are in spirit without being correspondingly pure in the spiritually condensed energy layers in our body right down to the cellular level, which is always in direct contact with our pure spirit energy, the more sick and unbalanced we risk being, without there being conventional psychological or medical explanations for this.

Think very carefully, therefore, about what you spend your time doing and who and what you are supporting in your life, (as mentioned in the chapter, *It Is Important To Support The Right People*) because it is vital for both your human and physical balance that you make the right choices in life - those that are as pure as they can possibly be and that also match your spiritual source. If you move too far away from your personal energy frequency and instead follow other people's truths, things often go wrong. From a pure frequency perspective, the spiritual-material energy in your body must match your pure spirit energy, to ensure balance on all levels, both in your body and in your life.

The Crystal energy in your body indicates what your life purpose is and how you are to use your Golden spiritual materialisation power in life. If you fail to follow the Crystal energy's instructions, you will create but with no specific, serious goal, meaning creation just for creation's sake, which could be seen as simple greed. You could end up just consuming and digesting just because you can, and not because it contributes something positive and constructive to either you or the world around you.

If you are pure, true and simple in your energy structure right back as far as your spiritual source, you will never try to take anything in that does not correspond to your life purpose. You will then be in a position to show your true self to others and as far as possible avoid resistance and blockages in your body and in your life.

The purity in the materially condensed energy structure depends at all times on the intention on the spirit level, which creates material structure and terrestrial expression.

If an object, idea or type of behaviour or manner of personal expression is charged with positivity and created with a positive goal in mind, the purity and positivity in the intention will be clearly reflected as purity in the object, idea, behaviour and expression and thus in the material energy and structure.

If, on the other hand, the object, idea, behaviour and personal expression are loaded with negativity and there are bad intentions behind them, this will express itself very clearly as a lack of purity in the energy in and around the object, idea, behaviour or personal expression. It really is that simple.

Some people are attracted to pure energy and others to various degrees of impure energy, depending on their spiritual standpoint in life and their spiritual purity right back to their source. Purity and impurity are always registered by those around us either on the conscious or subconscious levels, so there are few people here on Planet Earth who can make the excuse that they *did not know* that another person had negative or criminal intentions. If they are unaware of other people's negative intentions, it means that they *are not using* their own intuition regarding whom they choose to cooperate with, to frequent or to trust and believe.

Children and young people are, of course, subject to the decisions of others – but they must do everything they can to get away from evil, negativity and/or the criminality when they become adults or as soon as they can. Earth's Golden energy will, in the future, give extraordinary support on the energy front to help people in need who are not themselves to blame for their poverty and poor living conditions. These people will, out of pure gratitude, then begin to help others who need help and in that way, a positive developmental spiral will begin here on Planet Earth for the benefit of many, many people. Of course, as you know by now, the Crystal energy also has a finger in the pie as it is responsible for all human dharma in the New Time here on Earth.

THE PHYSICAL BODY IS SO MUCH MORE THAN YOU THINK

Our bodies are one big, cosmic, Golden, spiritually condensed library filled with masses of information, knowledge and insight about life, creation, spiritual and material energy, as well as the Cosmos and many other exciting things.

It is therefore important that you learn to listen to your body, because the more you listen to it, the more knowledge you will have about many different things in life without being able to explain these things simply by using your logic. You need to trust both yourself and the great cosmic library that is always with you and in which your pure spirit energy lives – namely, your physical body.

Most people gladly immerse themselves in books and externally sourced knowledge because they are interested in learning new things but if you only knew just how much essential knowledge about you, your life and your behaviour is contained in your body conduct, you would be astonished.

The person you are, and the physical body you have, are due to the fact that you are made of a very specific substance and you vibrate in a certain way, which can be expressed in the physical world in only one way, according to how your personal energy and your physical appearance were when you were born. Later in life, it was possible for you to adjust your personality, attitude and appearance in line with your development as a person and spiritual-material individual here on Planet Earth.

Maybe you have got much bigger muscles than was originally expected or have done really well in mathematics, even though you thought that languages were your strong point. You may also have had cosmetic surgery, which has significantly changed your adult appearance, etc. This has happened because you have changed your basic energy compared to where you were when you were born. Every person develops and changes in different consciousness directions in terrestrial life.

The only thing you *cannot* change in your body is the consciousness coding, located in the DNA in your cells, which relates to your dharma and your terrestrial life tasks. Because of your dharma you are here on Earth and it would be very strange if you suddenly changed your life purpose while you were in the middle of living it.

You cannot escape your dharma on the spiritual level unless you try to take your own life but even this will very rarely succeed for those who are predestined to do certain things. So, those planning to take an overdose to get out of here for good will find that the pills will suddenly not work as intended, or that the train is cancelled on the day they were going throw themselves under it. The Crystal and Golden energies are often there on the spot to 'adjust' things if something totally wrong is about to unfold here on Planet Earth, especially now, in the New Time when the two energies are cooperating on every matter.

CONNECT TO YOUR BODY ENERGY

If you try to connect with energies that are outside yourself in your surroundings or far out in the Cosmos somewhere, you will be moving the focus of your consciousness away from the force field in your own body. This means that you are forgetting to take care of your own energy because you cannot be simultaneously outwardly and inwardly focused. You therefore risk opening yourself up for other people and energies to occupy your body, your mind and/or your personal energy so that they can access your terrestrial materialisation power. This means that you will suddenly have to fight against unseen forces in your own body and your mind to succeed in life as you wish.

If you leave your body with your full consciousness to connect with an outside force or with another person's energy, you are leaving God's power and the materialisation power which is resident in your own body. By doing this, you could easily fall into *chaos*, which is the sum of all human imbalances both here on Earth and in the Cosmos.

Never give your terrestrial power away to someone or something that you do not trust and that does not know what it means to be a human being on Planet Earth in a physical body. Nor should you give your power away to other people who do not understand who you are and what type of energy and dharma you have. Always take responsibility for yourself, for your own energy and for whoever you allow into your personal energy field, your body or your aura.

It is not the direct contact with 'those back home' far out in the Cosmos that makes you who you are. Who you are and why you are here, is encoded in the deepest frequency level in your body energy right down to the cellular level, since the body with its spiritual-material energy structure acts as a complete reflection of your spirit energy. It is just a matter of how deeply you want to dig into your own body consciousness to get in touch with 'the real you' and your creative life impulse. The greater your power, the deeper you will dig to find yourself and your own truth.

It is not possible to get in touch with your terrestrial identity and your spiritually creative 'I' until you feel joy with yourself and with life. When you connect with your own bodily Golden energy, which is identical to your life force, you will get in contact with your spiritually creative 'I'. The prerequisite for this, however, is that you first have the Crystal energy integrated throughout your body, so you can control the Golden life force in your body in a balanced way.

So always remember to sort out the energy in your personal energy field by sending everyone else's energy back to them in the form in which you received it and then bring all your own energy back to you – and remember to clean the energy before taking it into your body.

If you have updated your personal energy by having an Aura-Transformation™, or if you were born with pure spirit energy in your aura in the form of an Indigo or Crystal aura, then do not take the energy back into your aura. Your aura will already be whole and serve solely as your terrestrial protection and personal radiance.

However, if you still have a soul aura, it is recommended that you pull all the energy that you have got back from other people into both your body and your aura, as the soul aura acts as an energetic extension of your body energy.

Now go into the cellular level in your body and sort out the energies in order to be sure that you only have your own energy in your body. If you feel that you are lacking energy, even though you have done your best to get your energy back from other people, you will have to recuperate the energy from the network of the people from whom you have pulled your energy back. Maybe these people have passed your energy on or shared it with others, because they have been inspired by you, or because they haven't been able to hold all the energy themselves.

It may also be appropriate to draw your energy back from all the places you have been, as well as from the situations and experiences you have been a part of. Last but not least, it may be appropriate to draw all your energy back from the planets in our solar system, as well as from other universes out in the Cosmos.

The anti-force may also have got a share in your personal energy if, in the past, you have been very angry or have thought a lot of negative thoughts and have behaved badly.

You can also focus on connecting with the Golden creation and creative energy in your body, which is only *your* energy and exclusively relates to *your* body and let the Golden energy spread into every cell in your entire body to create life and joy for the benefit of yourself and others.

This will help you to become really happy and filled with your own Golden spiritually condensed life energy in your body, which will be reflected out into your aura. Activating the Golden energy in your body in this way will not give you a Golden aura but it could appear to be so because the Golden energy will begin to radiate out from your body. You will however become much more terrestrially visible to those around you. This is the effect of connecting the Golden energy with the Crystal energy in your body.

If you have not yet been body-crystallised and your dharma and life tasks have not yet been activated at the cellular level in your body, then the activation of the Golden energy may cause you to become more physically visible but without you having access to your dharma in your body. Therefore you will not know what your life purpose is and could thus risk using your Golden materialisation power in a very inappropriate, unstructured and selfish manner in your life.

As I have said several times already as it is of paramount importance, you must first focus on integrating the Crystal energy in your body so that you can be responsible for your own body energy and life in a conscious and balanced way, before you start to activate the life-enhancing Golden energy. It is the Crystal-Golden energy, which is a combination of Crystal energy and Golden energy, that will best help you to realise your life purpose while at the same time helping you to feel vitality and life force. If you focus solely on realising your dharma in life, then life could very well seem quite dull if you do not give yourself the opportunity to feel happy about the way you spend your time.

The activation of the Golden energy in your body has the sole purpose of helping you to realise the things in life that you are born to do, as well as to inspire you, make you active and fill you with the joy of living.

SELF-BALANCING IS IMPORTANT

It is extremely important that you are able to balance your-self and your own energy in the Golden energy so that you are constantly making sure that you sort the energy when you are, or have been with other people. It is also important for you to remember to relax and recharge by sleeping, eating healthily and generally enjoying life

What is even more important, however, is that you are careful *not* to share your dharma and life task with others unless they have exactly the same life task in cooperation with you, for your dharma is *yours* in exactly the same way as your body is.

You are, of course, welcome to tell other people about your life task but if they have not yet found their way to their own life task, they may be inspired to do the exact same thing as you if you share every detail with them. If they have not yet got an idea of their own life task and yours sounds really exciting, perhaps they will feel inspired to do something similar, not because they want to steal your life task from you but because it is perhaps the most exciting thing they have heard about so far.

Do not, therefore, tempt others to follow in your tracks or to copy you if they have not yet finished the crystallisation in their own body, because their dharma will then not be available on the surface of their body ready to be realised. Their dharma will instead be hidden deep down on the cellular level, where it will lie in wait until their personal energy is ready to start carrying out their own life tasks.

It is only when the Golden energy begins to stir in the body in the part of the body energy that is crystallised that dharma gets the opportunity to escape from the body. The Crystal energy ensures that you hold your dharma and your respective voca-tions firmly in your body until the New Time Golden energy and power is activated and can help the Crystal energy to put the particular life tasks into operation at a high-frequency level. In the Golden Age, it is extremely important for Planet Earth that all initiatives taken by high-frequency people main-tain a high standard of consciousness. It has to be possible for everyone to be able to distinguish between initiatives taken by high-frequency people with New Time Golden energy who want to help Earth and the Whole, and initiatives taken by low-frequency people with Golden energy on the soul level who are only thinking about themselves.

If you are with other people who already have the New Time Golden energy activated in their bodies at Crystal level, then you are safe to relax and share your experiences and knowledge, without them misusing this to their own advantage.

On the other hand, if you are with people who have not yet had the Golden energy in the body activated on the Crystal level, you should be extra careful about how much Golden energy and joy of living you share with them and how much you implicate and involve them in your life and your dharma. They will often use the energy and insight to create career, economic and personal benefits exclusively for themselves instead of spreading the energy to others for the benefit of many people at once. Not that there is anything wrong in earning extra money but the New Time Golden energy is so much more than just that. It aims to help the Earth's entire population and the planet to evolve and move to the next level with help, as you know by now, from the Crystal energy.

Earth's spiritual life and materialisation power do not want you in any way to be exploited by other people so that you are unable to contribute to the Whole because you have not yet learned to distinguish between good people and the self-serving ones. The Earth force wants the maximum number of people here on Earth to be strong individuals who can help build many varying societies, cultures and countries in a balanced and respectful manner for the benefit of all and with room for everyone. It is therefore important that you take care of your own energy and constantly keep a balance in your life by, among other things, keeping yourself in balance and recharging your energy, so you are better able to help those around you to focus on the same goal.

So please allow me say it again - remember to keep your Golden energy and dharma inside your body and take them with you everywhere, in the same way as you do with your body. In this way, you will always have the strength to put your life tasks into operation when the timing is right. In fact, you will be extra-prepared to embark on new projects when the time comes, because you will have held onto the energy for so long that it feels like total liberation to finally be able to release that particular life task out of the body.

Self-balancing is therefore infinitely important for your sense of readiness when the time is finally right to do what you were born to do – that is to start living your dharma.

THE SIGNIFICANCE OF THE FOUR ELEMENTS IN OUR LIVES

Earth's matrix and frequency structure is first and foremost based on duality; that is to say, on the masculine and feminine energies which represent two opposing poles.

If both of these poles were totally pure in their energy, they would repel each other and never want to be united. This is because pure masculine energy and pure feminine energy have nothing in common in their purest forms. So when one of them moves outward, the other always moves inward – and it continues like this endlessly.

Consequently, to avoid segregation and separation in the energies here on Earth, everything that exists has both poles in it, which means that the masculine and feminine energies are present in everything that surrounds us in our lives on the spiritual, physical and terrestrial levels. This is because the two energies represent the creative power and creation in their totally pure form. Without the presence of these two energies, life cannot be created on our planet.

The two opposing energies are therefore intertwined, and together, they create a physical radiance and dynamic on the consciousness level that creates the basis for all development and creation on Earth. If this were not the case, no development would take place at all, because the energies in their purest forms always choose to follow the basic impulse that is within them, without the willingness and the ability to exchange energy and experience with each other unless they are forced to.

As a result, the evolution of Earth began millions of years ago with a focus first and foremost on uniting the two most simplified and basic creation impulses – the masculine and feminine energies – by putting pressure on them to unite on the survival level in order for them to be stronger together. If Earth's development had been started at a much higher level of consciousness, the two opposing energies would have come up with countless intelligent excuses for avoiding each other, and then there would not have been life on our planet today.

The masculine and feminine energies are therefore united exclusively on the physical level here on Earth to ensure their *own* survival. This is how the balance energy found its way to Earth.

The pure masculine and the pure feminine energies are therefore each exclusively focused on maintaining their own internal state of balance, which inherently cannot be done. From a purely consciousness perspective, it is impossible for a solitary energy to achieve balance within itself. The concept of balance requires that there is a minimum of two energies present in order to create a balance between the energies. So when people focus on creating a balance within themselves, it is always done primarily between the masculine and feminine energies in their consciousness and their bodies. After that, the balancing process moves quite naturally to the next level, where we find the element energies.

The element energies consist of the elements of fire, water, earth and air, which represent four different types of consciousness and energy forms in different types of balance and strength relationships. Like the masculine and feminine energies, the four elements exist everywhere on Earth and in Earth's energy, as well as in all human beings, animals and nature. It is very much the elements which contribute to shaping the manifestation of and the radiance that surrounds everything that is created - people, animals, material objects, thoughts, feelings, ideas, etc.

When it comes to the four elements in everyday life, we humans experience them most clearly through our contact with others. The four elements are of paramount importance to how we experience being with other people. If we do not master our own personal element combination and if we are not conscious of our own way of expressing ourselves, we are not always aware of the effect we have on other people, because they may well have a different element combination. There is therefore a huge amount of useful knowledge and human insight hidden behind the concept of *the four elements* that many people would benefit greatly from knowing about in their dealings with other people; knowledge that should be deep-rooted in everyone but rarely is.

Knowledge about the four elements belongs to the most basic and effective insight it is possible to acquire in a terrestrial framework in the Golden Age, both in terms of specific knowledge about the elements on the physical and material level and also on the consciousness level. When we humans understand the importance of the different element combinations, and we know how to master them and use them as communication tools, it is much easier to communicate with others. It will also be much easier for our bodies to cooperate with our consciousness if we want to change our lives, personalities, etc. This is because our bodies know in detail about the nature of the elements, since they themselves consist of the four elements right down to the cellular level. Consequently, the body as a *whole* is usually much more cooperative in any process of change when the four elements are involved. If learning is merely a cerebral process, it will lack the power and impact of the four elements, as when they are involved in any process, the whole body listens.

If, therefore, you belong to that very large group of people who are often adversely affected by the personality and behaviour of others – especially if they are different from you – maybe you should start thinking about the importance of the four elements. Knowledge of the four elements can in fact help you to understand and balance your own energy better when you are interacting with other people. Above all, you will understand that the people concerned might be behaving as they do, not because they do not like you but simply because they have a particular element combination.

Understanding the four elements thus represents the most simple way to relate to other people here on Earth and it is through the use of the elements of fire, water, earth and air that we in the Golden Age will experience the greatest development on the physical, spiritual and human levels for the benefit of ourselves, the planet and all mankind.

In nature, the elements represent the four fundamental forces which are behind all interactions on Earth and in the rest of the universe and from which all other forces can be derived. The four elements will therefore have great importance in the Golden Age in society, where there will be even more emphasis on creating optimal natural force solutions for industry, for the heating of private homes, etc. Therefore, in the Golden Age, the four elements will not only promote development on the personal consciousness level but also throughout the whole of society.

BALANCE ON ALL LEVELS

As already stated, the four elements are essential to all physical life but it is just as important for you to have them integrated into your consciousness and personality. This is because they will help you to create wholeness and balance around your personal radiance and also in your interaction and cooperation with other people both at work and in private. Furthermore, insight into the differences between the elements will help you to better understand those around you, enabling you to communicate with them in a way that they can understand. This, in turn, creates the basis for greater understanding and fewer disappointments in your dealings with others.

The four elements are represented in each and every person and in various combinations with different proportions of balance and strength. These combinations of elements can be read in our faces, bodies, behaviour, speech, movement and radiance.

The four elements represent the following:

Fire represents your personal drive, force and inner fire.

Water represents your personal flow and your ability to remain in balance under all conditions.

Earth represents your personal expression, i.e. attitude and personal structure and your physical framework in everyday life.

Air represents your various forms of insight, from common sense to specific knowledge on various levels, your knowledge of human nature, your inspiration, creativity and vision.

The combination of the four elements translates into 15 broad personality profiles which are all described in a book co-written by my husband and me, "Be a Conscious Leader in Your Own Life", currently available in Danish and Swedish.

You can read more about the four elements on **www.fourelement profile.eu**, where you can also read about our courses, workshops and lectures on the elements.

One way of bringing balance into your personal energy and your life in the Golden Age is by understanding the four elements and their meaning in connection with all life – and especially with your own life.

∞ ∞ ∞ ∞ ∞ ∞ ∞ ∞ ∞

The balance between the masculine and feminine energies is also crucially important regarding whether you feel balance in your life, especially in your energy system and your radiance. Many believe, mistakenly, that the masculine and feminine energies are identical to the male and female energies. However, this is not so. The energies are not gender-specific and therefore have no impact on our body types and physical appearance.

Rather, the masculine and feminine energies relate to our radiance and energy fields and are therefore magnetically contingent. They impact on our radiance, behaviour and personal attractiveness in relation to those around us.

On the spirit level, pure feminine energy represents the inner core of pure knowledge and insight, inner peace, overview, stasis and the ability to hold one's own and others' energies together and to stand firm and be tenacious. However, it is extremely vulnerable without the presence of masculine energy.

This is because masculine energy represents external energy

and the membrane located around the core of feminine energy. The purpose of masculine energy is to communicate with the outside world and defend the feminine energy. It therefore possesses great drive, an eminent adaptability and the desire to be in constant motion in order to be alert and prepared for unexpected experiences and/or hostile attacks from outside.

Very briefly, masculine energy represents the will, while feminine energy represents capability and resourcefulness. Will and ability are two opposite poles and yet they complement each other. It is essential to balance these opposites in yourself in order to create as balanced an outer manifestation as you possibly can as a human being. If your will is stronger than your capability and resourcefulness, you will not succeed. If your capability is greater than your will, you will often find it difficult to set anything in motion. The balance between these two seeming dichotomies is therefore the key to succeeding and moving forward in life.

You can read much more about all this in my book "Balance on All Levels with the Crystal and Indigo Energies", where the masculine and feminine energies are described in detail in connection with having an AuraTransformation™. An AuraTransformation™ is a permanent consciousness upgrading of an adult's aura, energies and radiance.

∞ ∞ ∞ ∞ ∞ ∞ ∞ ∞ ∞

Apart from having balance between the fundamental energies here on Earth, it is very important for people's personal well-being that they have balance in their bodies, couple relationships, families and immediate personal circles as well as at work and in the community. Some also strive to bring balance on the spiritual level here on Earth and between the planets in our solar system and out in the closer realms of the universe and in the Cosmos. How far-reaching the need for balance in a person's life is depends very much on their consciousness perspective and capacity.

None of the areas mentioned should be overlooked, however, when focusing on creating personal Crystal-Golden balance in life, as all imbalances will eventually come tumbling out of the closet, for all to see, when something is not as it should be.

This is not because there are earth-shattering faults in those people who are in a temporary imbalance. The purpose of visibility is solely to get them to act quickly on a given imbalance so that balance can be (re)created at once. That is how it is here on Earth in the spiritual-material energy sphere; because if any imbalance is not taken care of immediately, it will spread like wildfire and you suddenly find you have many other imbalances, which will then also have to be addressed.

It is similar to not cleaning up or keeping track of things over a long period of time. Things can get out of hand so quickly that suddenly, there are not just a few things to fix but layers of imbalances that have built up over a long period – and these imbalances may well have begun to merge into one another so you can make neither head nor tail of what is going on – nor of your own energy.

So we should actually thank Earth's Golden energy for making all sorts of imbalances visible so that we can start doing something about them, because if we do not see the imbalances clearly in our daily lives, we often cannot find the best, rapid solution to problems. Earth's high-frequency Golden energy prefers correct, fast, joyful solutions to all kinds of imbalances.

Balance on all levels is Earth's motto in the Golden Age, and by all levels, I mean the earthly, the physical and the spiritual levels.

CONSCIOUSNESS-DEVELOPING RELATIONSHIPS

Here on Earth, there are currently three extraordinary con-sciousness-developing couple relationship types, which depend on the couple's age and where the couple finds itself from a consciousness perspective. The three couple relationship types create different forms of development for the couple as well as for the individual parties:

Soul mates

Consciousness mates

Spirit mates

In addition, there are four extraordinarily significant conscious-ness relationships between people who are not in a couple rela-tionship with each other and here we also find consciousness mates:

Soul friends

Consciousness mates

Spirit family

Source duals

Purely energetically, none of the afore-mentioned relationships can be equated with one another because they belong to different spheres of consciousness and on different levels of conscious-ness, on which I will elaborate in this chapter.

∞ ∞ ∞ ∞ ∞ ∞ ∞ ∞ ∞

Soul energy belongs in Earth's and the solar system's old rein-carnation and karma system, where all relationships between people, including couple relationships, have always been agreed from one life to the next. This means that the soul couple has been predestined to meet in one or more lives as part of their development from both the consciousness and the human per-spective.

By meeting repeatedly in different lives on the soul level, the couple have had the opportunity to create a deeper relationship with each other in order to gain a more thorough knowledge of each other's often very different types of consciousness. They thus feel at home and comfortable in each other's company because they have known each other in many lives and know what to expect of each other, even though their karma and destiny may have changed radically from one life to the next.

It is through the reincarnation system on the soul level that, for example, Mr. Mars and Mrs. Venus have had the opportunity of meeting as love partners here on Earth; otherwise, the two very different types of consciousness would never have managed to accept each other's existences. So it is definitely not without reason that people here on Earth have not been able to access their full spirit potential on the soul level. If they had known each other's true identities from the beginning, they may well have loathed each other instead of loving each other as agreed. Now, however, they have had the opportunity to get used to each other's energies over many thousands of years and perhaps even integrate energy from each other thanks to their many predetermined lives together.

The soul-reincarnation system was a truly efficient system for integrating different types of consciousness into Earth's population but it was also a very slow system. A lot of time, which could otherwise have been used to expand the consciousness of those ready for it, was spent managing the system.

As time passed, several different types of consciousness, from both within and outside of our solar system, wanted to have the possibility of living here on Earth with the sole purpose of testing their insight and abilities with regard to consciousness on the visible material level. Earth, as said earlier, is one of the few places in the Cosmos where spiritual and condensed visible material energy are in close contact with each other. Having the opportunity of living a terrestrial human life here is a unique opportunity for many external consciousnesses to show to themselves and to the highest power who they are and what they can do. There are all kinds of opportunities to improve your consciousness CV here on Earth.

However, many people with a broad consciousness seem to outgrow the various systems if they start to get bored. If there are no challenges or interesting opportunities for expansion and personal development in their immediate vicinity, they begin instead to search for new ideas and possibilities deep within themselves or out in the Cosmos. What happens then?

What happens is what happened on the soul level back in the 1960s, when the Uranus energy with its New-Age-inspired wave of energy tried to encourage people to think outside the box. A large number of ultra-spiritual people and people with an inherent cosmic insight regarding technology, art, design, architecture, human rights, politics, etc. suddenly discovered that they were not obliged to have access to their full consciousness potential on the soul level. They therefore tried to break with the established norms and frameworks and thus attained access to much more of their own spiritual consciousness and insight within their respective disciplines and areas of interest. This was done either by thinking abstractly and completely outside of the box, or by taking euphoriants.

The consequence was that the soul system was gradually closed down during the period 1987-1995, when the Indigo energy appeared on Earth. This is because Indigo people have no soul energy in their auras and energy systems. They are here to get rid of the soul energy and the parental generation's established and often very limited thought patterns. We can see this when we look at the often transgressive behaviour of many Indigo children and young adults, which was particularly visible out in society from 2000 onwards.

The growing presence of ADHD is largely due to the need to break with the existing framework on the soul level and create some more individually-based frameworks better adapted to the needs of the individual. This is because Indigo children and young adults do not feel at home in the soul energy in the same way as their parents' generation does. They feel stifled and often react by getting mental and emotional claustrophobia from the limited development opportunities found on the soul level. As a result, they can react in very violent and uncontrolled ways in order to get a sense of themselves and their own needs. Something similar happens for many adults who have been born on the soul level with an inherent Indigo energy stored somewhere in their consciousness.

The soul energy has nothing constructive to offer to the dynamic and transforming consciousness universe of Indigo people.

∞ ∞ ∞ ∞ ∞ ∞ ∞ ∞ ∞

On the Indigo level, it is possible to meet your consciousness mate and it is indeed possible to meet several on your personal path of development. Consciousness mates can be both domestic partners and friends of both sexes. The energetic similarity between consciousness mates arises in connection with their personal development in a terrestrial framework, which is not the same as saying that they are identical in spirit.

A consciousness mate relationship is not always sexually and physically focused and the relationship may, as mentioned, express itself as a deep friendship or a very short and intense love affair that often fizzles out. Even very small differences can separate consciousness mates from each other in their terrestrial lives and this can often occur in unpleasant and negative ways, completely out of proportion to the extent of the diversity.

A person's spirit mate is quite simply the other part of the spiritual energy with which the person initially came into being, on the spirit level, at the dawn of time at the moment of the great cosmic cell division. Spirit mates thus have identical consciousness structures because of their common origin in the spirit and may already have met each other on the soul level. They are rarely conscious here of their deep interconnectedness in the spirit, unless it has been predetermined that they should know this.

Spirit mates have a deep and fervent love for one another and an often inexplicable sense of internal interconnectedness, which soul mates and consciousness mates could never experience in the same way, no matter how deeply they may love each other.

Consciousness mates and spirit mates can initially appear to be very similar. The difference is simply in how fast imbalances arise in the relationship, since it is basically inordinately difficult for spirit mates to disagree about anything at all. On the other hand, consciousness mates fall out easily.

To date, there are very few people on Earth who have met up with their spirit mate. The overall energy on Earth is, however, fast approaching the consciousness level from which it is possible for spirit mates to completely accommodate their own and each other's energies completely on the everyday consciousness level so that they can begin to live together as a couple. In order to accommodate your spirit mate's energy you must be able to accommodate yourself and your own energy. Otherwise, it is not possible to relate to a different version of your own energy and consciousness in everyday life – namely, your spirit mate's energy.

If the spirit mates meet each other too soon, they risk being completely engrossed in each other, especially on the sexual front, so that they are unable to work constructively in relationships with other people. So the prerequisite for spirit mates being allowed to meet on the terrestrial level is that each of them is in perfect balance with her/himself and with the outside world, because they have a joint life task that they have to put into practice. By combining and integrating each other's energies, they will in act be more than twice as strong as a couple on the consciousness level, which means that they have an opportunity of being extraordinarily successful with the tasks they have to carry out.

Thus there is a seriousness attached to spirit mates meeting each other here on Earth.

When a spirit mate couple meet, they often come from two different poles and worlds in their physical lives but not in their respective spirits. By bringing together two people with a completely identical spiritual consciousness but with very different life experiences, the possibility is created for God's power to be able to materialise the spirit energy on Planet Earth with far greater force than was ever possible before.

As mentioned, spirit mates have the same spiritual source and come from the same cell division of consciousness. However, all cells in the Cosmos were not created simultaneously. Some cell divisions took place at a much later moment in time than others. In essence, everyone belongs together in the spirit if we trace all cell divisions on the consciousness level back to the source. However, not everyone is able to feel the interconnectedness on the terrestrial material level.

Every spirit mate relationship is always a piece of a spirit mate relationship on a higher level of consciousness. The way this has to be understood is that once it becomes possible for people here on Earth to live with much greater consciousness than now, those who are spirit mates today will be merged into one joint consciousness that will then reside in a single human body.

The energy of the two spirit mates, which will be merged into one greater consciousness in one body, will then join together with another fused dual-energy in another body. Neither of these two new larger consciousnesses in the two bodies will ever imagine that, sometime back in Earth's evolutionary history, they were split into two separate energies that were divided between two different human bodies.

Everyone consists of two dual-energies which, at an earlier stage in their consciousness development and in a previous life, were divided between two human bodies. So it is perfectly correct to say that you can never separate the energy of spirit mates, because they are destined to merge into one and the same body at a later stage in the evolution of Earth's consciousness.

Spirit mate energies will always merge when it is time to take a quantum leap to the next level of consciousness in their common development. God's power has ensured that the correct cell divisions will join together again when the Cosmos, sometime in the future, returns to its spiritual source, otherwise disorder could easily arise in the system.

When spirit mate consciousnesses merges in the future, the consciousness of the two spirit mates will join together to be part of a larger spirit mate energy, which also consists of two other spirit mate energies that have also merged into one common spirit mate energy.

This is what spiritual development basically consists of – leading all spiritual consciousness back to its source when the spirit at some future time has acquired so much cosmic knowledge and experience in the material and condensed energy sphere that God's power will be able to lift itself to a new and higher level of consciousness. A new Big Bang will then take place, focusing on a completely different type of consciousness development for the benefit of the evolution of God's power on the cosmic level. So even on God's level, there is a continuous integration of new energies and insights taking place, just as there is on Planet Earth.

As for spirit mates searching for each other here on Earth, they can easily happen to meet partners who match their energy 70%, 80% and 90%. This happens in order to gradually prepare their energy systems to meet their own energy in another body which matches their spirit energy 100%.

∞ ∞ ∞ ∞ ∞ ∞ ∞ ∞ ∞

Soul friends, like soul mates, are individuals who have been together through many lives, which is why they have a thorough knowledge of each other's energy structures and personal development behind the scenes. However, they are rarely aware of this on the everyday-consciousness level. They just feel that they belong together in some way, which causes them to value the friendship very highly.

Their shared history and consciousness development, like that of soul mates, has been agreed from one life to another as part of the soul reincarnation system in our solar system. They have often wanted to meet again and again in different lives because, due to their in-depth knowledge of each other, they are much better at giving each other support on the human and emotional level than other people.

When it comes to spirit families, they have exactly the same function on the spirit level that soul friends have on the soul level. The big difference is that members of spirit families are often very conscious that they have a deep relationship on the spirit level and that they have been together through many lives both here on Planet Earth and in other universes. Their energy bond and interconnectedness is not limited to this solar system.

The reason why they are called family members is that, in the future here on Earth, they will, in many cases, replace the physical and/or biological family. The spirit family will thus become the one that a lot of people will spend most of their time with, because their mutual spiritual interconnectedness is so great that they want to see each other often. Some people will be lucky enough to have identical biological family and spirit family members, although this is far from being the case in all families. Often, the spirit family will only consist of selec- ted biological family members and not of the whole family. In addition, new spirit family members will come from outside as spirit family members begin to meet up with one another other as they move through life.

Spirit family members often develop in a significantly positive way in each other's company on all levels. So the human strength and personal skills that parents usually help their children to develop while they are growing up can be acquired to a great extent from the spirit family if there should be anything missing in their personalities.

Members of spirit families support each other in an extra-ordinary way, by being together in twos, threes, fours, etc. and/or the whole family at the same time. So they operate largely as an ordinary family with the crucial difference being that they also follow and support each other on the spirit level as it is in the spirit that they are connected. However, they do not arise from the same cell division as spirit mates do.

∞ ∞ ∞ ∞ ∞ ∞ ∞ ∞ ∞

A source dual is a dharma and life task focused relationship that can take place between people of all ages as long as they have the same overall source in the spirit on a higher level of cons-ciousness. You could say that they belong in different places in the consciousness layers and the development chain – a bit like cousins belonging to the same family.

So when their consciousnesses merge one day in the future, it will happen on a much higher level of consciousness, where many other source duals are also part of the same merger. Thanks to the merger, the source duals will together form a much higher consciousness, where all previously divided spirit conscious-nesses are on an equal footing with one another, because they have originally consisted of the same substance.

The source-dual merging process can to a large degree be equated with the spirit mate mergers that will take place in the future, because source duals are actually spirit mates who are cooperating across the system. They are really spirit mates but just not with each other. However, it is quite certain that their consciousnesses will merge at a later time and it is often because of their great similarity in energy structure that they feel drawn to cooperate with each other and share insights and experience.

In the terrestrial sphere, source duals can easily find themselves on different levels of consciousness, yet come from the same overall spiritual source, as we all of course originate from the same spiritual source, back in the origins of the Cosmos.

To summarise briefly, spirit mates originate from the same cell and cell division and function as a dual energy in relation to each other. They complement each other and therefore work together best as partners here on Planet Earth, rather than being friends or siblings who are not supposed to merge their energies together in the terrestrial sphere. When spirit mates join together and cooperate, their joint power grows and strengthens to more than double.

Source duals are *not* spirit mates and they work across the system instead of coming from the same spiritual platform as spirit mates do. Source duals have life tasks equivalent to the scale of the life tasks of spirit mates but their energies are not complementary like those of spirit mates. However, they are more alike in their human and mental energy structures, but their joint power does not grow monumentally as the joint power of spirit mates does.

If you want to know more about spirit mates, I recommend that you read the book "Spirit Mates – The New Time Relationship", co-written by my husband and me, which is very a easy read.

WHAT CAN YOU CONTRIBUTE?

Although openness and honesty are among the most important human qualities on the Crystal level, these characteristics are even more important in your relationships with others in the Golden energy. Here, there are many doors which will close for you on your way forward in life if you try to move in the wrong direction, because you are not being honest with yourself and other people about your own desires and needs.

Openness and honesty are also important in your communication with other people if you want to realise those things in life that mean the most to you. Even in relation to people with whom you are not on the same wavelength, or who you do not like, it is important to be honest. You will thereby avoid the people in question having hidden expectations of you that they will then try to make you fulfil. If they know very clearly that you will not let them into your life, both of you get the chance to go your separate ways in order to explore new possibilities in life.

By being open and honest with yourself and others, the general development of consciousness on Earth will also be more rapid and we will all benefit because then there will be no need to spend a lot of time clearing up misunderstandings and resolving conflicts. So do be open and honest with yourself and others if you wish to reach your important goals more quickly.

Many spiritual people mistakenly believe that it is the New Time energy that changes people's lives but this is just not the case. The New Time energy, in many instances, enables people to see clearly in a new way and on a new level, depending on whether it is 'New Time' Indigo, Crystal or Golden energy. In the light of that knowledge, people change their lives themselves if they feel they need to. There are of course billions of people around the world who will not change their lives or their consciousness every time a new consciousness influx to Earth opens up, simply because they cannot feel the energy in their systems.

These people who do not feel anything in their bodies and the rest of their energy systems are usually focused principally on the material and visible factors in life. They would therefore not belong to the category of sensitive and intuitive spiritual people. So if they are to be motivated to change their lives and behaviour, it is best done by convincing them using visible, tangible evidence and results that can be clearly seen and understood on the physical and terrestrial levels. Consequently, all spiritual people do themselves and those around them, as well as the Whole, a huge favour by being extra visible with their personal energies. In this way, they increase the likelihood of bringing a more tangible influence to bear on those people who belong in the heavy material and non-spiritual consciousness here on Earth, enabling them to begin to change their lives and behaviour in accordance with the values of the Golden Age.

Many people are convinced that you have to live in a very specific way, to have completed certain spiritual initiations, to have a strong religious belief or to live in silence and meditate to be a spiritual person. In truth, however, being spiritual does not require very much. Being spiritual cannot be described briefly but the hallmark of most spiritual people is that they are often very loving, truth-loving and accommodating in their relations with other people, without renouncing their own inner convictions in order to adapt to other people's truths.

Many spiritual people focus more on helping and supporting other people to make contact with their own spirit and power and in becoming better people, rather than focusing on the material values in life. In addition, they are open in different ways to the existence of a higher divine power that cannot be seen with the naked eye. They not only *believe* that God exists – they *know* he does.

When a spiritual person knows that there is a greater power and a meaning to life, they automatically feel more confident and comfortable. It is extremely important to communicate this security to other people who do not know what to believe in life or who have given up believing in something bigger. By giving them hope, they simultaneously feel life and joy being activated in their minds and bodies, which can contribute to them beginning to attract positive experiences instead of negative experiences.

So you can really make a positive difference here for many people you meet who have no greater purpose in life than just to live an ordinary life. Encourage them to do something good for others, because that will give them something to live for – namely good experiences and gratitude from those around them. In other words, life will have some meaning for them.

Remember also to pay attention to what you are thinking, because your thoughts function as open and closed doors in relation to what is possible in your life and in the lives of those close to you. Positive thoughts open doors and negative thoughts close doors.

This is something that you can beneficially communicate to the people you encounter. In fact, very few people are aware of this and they are often astonished when they see what benefits they can reap from positive thinking. Help them by setting a positive spin going in the lives of other people if you feel that they are open to it and need it and they cannot get started on their own. However, they must make the choice to do this themselves.

The cost in resources on your side will be so little and you will thereby have contributed to other people on Planet Earth beginning little by little to cooperate with God's underlying invisible power for the benefit of themselves and those around them.

When you are focused on having balance in your own life, it is not certain that your way of balancing matches other people's ways of balancing. Maybe you need some different things in your life for you to feel in balance from the things that other people may need in their lives, especially when it comes to inner balance.

Our inner balance is not always visible to others and it is important to be aware that there is no set formula for how balancing can take place in a human life, either on the inside or the outside. So do not judge others based on your first impressions of them unless you have a strong intuition that tells you that you should stay away from them. Perhaps they are not as accustomed as you are to balance in relationships with the outside world, whereas they may have perfectly fine balance when they are at home.

Balance cannot be measured and judged on the basis of a general social assessment but rather according to how you are as a person and individual when you are with others and when you do certain things in life. The overriding consideration must therefore be, that you feel comfortable with the things you do; it may well be that others do not feel similarly comfortable with the same things. For example, not everyone feels good about skydiving but those whose hobby it is are filled with a sense of freedom and personal well-being which often translates into increased internal and external balance.

That some people seem more balanced than others is often due to others feeling comfortable when they are with them because there is a good match between the parties. It does not mean, however, that everyone else enjoys their company, and maybe they do not have more balance in life than many others do but instead radiate calmness and joy, which tends to relax most people.

So make room in your life to accommodate other people, each with their different forms of personal balance and personalities – it creates life and good experiences and increases your consciousness in various areas. You can always focus on your own inner balance when you are alone, where you can take your time to digest the impressions and impulses you may have in the company of others. If you are always focused on keeping your own personal balance intact without taking in new impressions from the outside world and without getting involved in other people's perhaps unbalanced lives, you have no chance whatsoever of increasing your personal consciousness and contributing to the evolution of Earth. If this is the case, you really do not have any reason to be here on this planet.

You are on an equal footing with every other person as an active part of the overall integration process here on Earth at this time and therefore you have both a human obligation and a consciousness obligation to contribute to the Whole with the best efforts you can, by being open to new impulses and by sharing your personal strengths and knowledge with others.

THE IMPORTANT ANSWERS LIE WITHIN YOU

Life is obviously not only about thinking of others. It is most important to think of yourself too. Being with others and exchanging energy and knowledge is important so that you can develop optimally as a person and expand your consciousness horizons.

Maybe you do not need to learn a lot of practical knowledge from others because you do not need it to carry out your life task but you can learn how others think by listening to them. This insight may be needed in many contexts out in the world where you might suddenly be able to help others who need precisely the knowledge to which you have been able to gain access, without you being able to use it yourself. In this way, you become a kind of spiritual guide in a physical body that disseminates useful information to others.

When you listen to yourself and look for answers inside, it is important that first and foremost you listen to the answers that come from the deepest layers of cellular consciousness in your body. Here you will find answers to all the questions that deal with yourself and your own life. If you only listen to your brain, your heart or your gut feeling to get answers to the important questions in your life, you will most often only get partial answers and not the whole truth. This necessitates full crystallisation in your body and activation of the New Time Golden energy in your body consciousness.

You can read about the body crystallisation process in my books "The Crystal Human and the Crystallization Process Part I" and "Part II". The body crystallisation process is a long-term consciousness upgrading of bodily energy, which takes at least as long as it takes for an unborn child to be created in the womb

– and it often takes even longer for adults to crystallise in the body as in most cases it feels like being born again into their existing body.

Even though everyone originally comes from the same spiritual source way back in time, we do not all have the same truth in life. We therefore do not share the same opinions or ways of living here on Planet Earth, where condensed spirit energy and materialism can be expressed in billions of different ways and at very different frequencies through our bodies and minds. You should therefore not listen solely to what other people say, even if you trust them implicitly. It is extremely important that you always listen within yourself and to your own body before accepting or rejecting information that others may share with you, so that you do not automatically make their truth into your truth.

You could try spending some time in nature or making yourself one with the Earth force to get the answers to the things that you are unsure about in your life. Nature and the Earth force in fact have no mental energy or emotion to try and influence you in the same way as people do. In nature, your body energy gets an opportunity to unfold exactly as it needs to, unless you are surrounded by other people with a different life agenda from yours.

When you go out into nature, your spirit energy has the possibility of completely penetrating into your body in a natural way without external and/or human limitations. This corresponds to a body crystallisation in miniature and a simultaneous mini-activation of the Golden energy within your body. You can usefully spend a lot of time in nature if you need answers to important questions in life that only you can answer, because nature is you and your body's best friend when you need to verify your truth.

One day, when the Crystal energy is fully integrated into your body and you are completely crystallised, it will be time to activate the Golden energy in your cells, so that you can get direct access to your own life force and can begin to put your dharma into practice. The Golden energy helps your body to maintain a constant rhythm, so that all the life tasks you have lying in storage in your body automatically emerge from the system when it is time for you to bring them to fruition.

WHAT HAPPENS TO YOUR AURA
IN THE GOLDEN ENERGY?

When the body energy has got to the point where it is completely crystallised and the Golden energy is activated on the Crystal level of the body, it is not pure Golden energy that is the result off this activation. Rather, it is the Crystal-Golden energy that expresses itself and spreads throughout the physical body because it is spiritually dense and material in its energy structure. The aura, however, which is much lighter in its energy structure than the body, will continue being a soul aura, an Indigo aura or Crystal aura, depending on which consciousness dimension you belong to personally.

This can mean that your body energy can actually end up having to be of a much higher frequency and thus much more 'intelligent' than your aura if you have both Crystal-Golden energy in your body and the soul aura that most adults have today. This could have happened, for example, because you have exercised really hard and lived extra healthily, or because you have been doing yoga for many years, and so on. In this way, you will have first integrated the Crystal energy in your body and then later activated the correspondingly high-frequency Golden energy all the way down to the cellular level in your body. The result is that you will now have the Crystal-Golden energy integrated and activated in your body but your personal radiance is still on the soul level, meaning that you will not have the same development opportunities in life that people with Indigo and Crystal auras have.

As you already know, all of today's children and young people are born with a Crystal aura. Adults who have a soul aura can upgrade to a Crystal aura by having an AuraTransformation™.

If the difference between the level of consciousness in the body and the aura is too great, it can make adults totally fanatical when it comes to diet and exercise, without them being able to explain why. It is actually difficult for them to find inner peace and balance in their energy systems if they are fully crystallised and energetically updated in their body but not in their aura and personal radiance.

Soul people with crystallised body energy often do not feel at their best in everyday life and they are often dissatisfied with themselves if they do not push themselves and their bodies to the limit. It is only when they are pushing their bodies to the pain threshold or exposing it to extremely harsh physical efforts that large amounts of endorphins are released in their bodies, which gives them a temporary feeling of happiness, one which matches the energy level in their body on the spirit level but unfortunately not the energy level in their aura on the soul level.

In fact, hard training is often the only way in which adults with a soul aura can come into direct contact with the high-fre quency spirit energy in the body where the frequency-related fluctuation rate is much higher than in the aura. Then they often feel rejuvenated.

∞ ∞ ∞ ∞ ∞ ∞ ∞ ∞ ∞

If you are young and were born in the period from 1995 to 2004, when all children were born with an Indigo aura or with a mixed Indigo-Crystal aura, or if you are an adult and have had an AuraTransformation™ at the time when the Indigo aura was the most 'upgraded' aura structure you could get, then your aura will automatically upgrade itself to Crystal level when you are ready for this in your life. The upgrading of the aura will happen much faster than normal if you exercise a lot and eat and live very healthily. You can read about this in my books "Balance on All Levels with the Crystal and Indigo Energies" and "The Crystal Human and the Crystallization Process Part I" and "Part II".

All today's children and young people who were born with an Indigo and/or a Crystal aura and all adults who have had their aura structure upgraded to either Indigo or Crystal level by having an AuraTransformation™ will always be able, using their own power and through their own will, to begin to upgrade their aura structure and body energy to the 'next level' on the spirit level, both in the Golden energy and further into the future.

Adults who were born with a soul aura, however, cannot do that because their personal consciousness has to pass from the soul level across the Indigo transformation bridge to the spirit level on the other side. They must renounce their previous spiritual grounding along the way. When we humans make the transition for the first time from the soul level to the spirit level with our full consciousness, it feels in many ways like dying and starting all over again with a new life in our existing bodies and with a new, stronger personal radiance. This is something that the children and young people born with Indigo and Crystal auras will never ever get to experience in their physical life on Earth, as they are all born on the spirit level.

The transition between the soul energy and the spirit energy began to take place around the start of this millennium. It is therefore, for adults, a question of personal choice whether to live on the soul level or the spirit level.

∞ ∞ ∞ ∞ ∞ ∞ ∞ ∞ ∞

In the Golden Age, everyone who has a Crystal aura will have an aura that is continuously more compressed as they become ready to learn what they have come to Earth to do, after which it will be time for them to begin using what they have learned to help others and to contribute towards improving society and Planet Earth.

If you have a Crystal aura, it will therefore slowly begin to 'close' all by itself, so that you will just register external impressions in your energy system *without* beginning to process them as if they were your own impulses and impressions. However, this is a very prolonged consciousness-related process on the personal level which can take many years to complete and it is a process that you can by no means force or push through just because you want to. If you still have even the smallest thing to learn or recognise in order to carry out your future life tasks in a strengthened and responsible manner, the Crystal aura compression process will wait until the time is right.

Furthermore, it is of paramount importance that you develop a super-strong personal and energy-related discernment in life so that the Crystal aura compression process can start by itself when the Golden energy is finally fully deployed on the Crystal level in the body. This discernment will enable you to quickly assess other people's personalities and energies, so that you do not run the risk of suddenly being tricked by energy-rich people who have a different agenda from your own, just as things start to flow really well for you in the Crystal-Golden energy.

Some spiritual people perceive this very strong and compressed aura, which the Crystal aura finally becomes, as being a Diamond aura but Diamond energy has nothing to do with what our future aura will look like. The Diamond energy is solely related to the consciousness structure of the body, which I will only briefly touch on in this book, as I wish to concentrate primarily on providing information on the Crystal-Golden energy and the Golden energy.

WHAT HAPPENS WITH THE BODY ENERGY?

All conscious people on Earth have the task of integrating their spirit energy in the body and finding their way to their own personal energy frequency and power to achieve personal balance and to carry out their dharma. However, there are plenty of people on this planet who do not have this latent possibility in their energy systems because they come from outside the solar system and do not know about Earth's energy from within. Therefore, they do not feel at home in the Golden energy which is now ready and beginning to spring up everywhere on Earth.

Until the end of the Mayan calendar in December 2012, the Golden energy was encapsulated in Earth's interior. This was due to the presence of many external entities and individuals who had taken up residence in human bodies everywhere on Earth and it was unable to express itself on its original, powerful, high-frequency energy level without creating problems for these visitors. So up until now, the Golden energy has only had the possibility of expressing its enormous creative power and vitality through nature and animals. Now, however, it is the turn of us humans to integrate and activate the Golden energy in our own bodies.

Human structures and body structures, which are not a purely earthly phenomena but rather a compromise consisting of diverse energies and impulses from the other planets in our solar system for which the Uranus energy has responsibility, are thus going to have to pass a test of their strength. How much can the human body withstand on the consciousness level and how much consciousness is there room for in the human body, especially in the brain, without it affecting human memory?

These are extremely important questions that will have great significance and will get great attention in the Golden Age, when talented scientists around the world will take both the body and the spirit into account in all their research, as if it were the most natural thing in the world.

New thinking and abstract thinking regarding exploration of the human body and its potential for development will come strongly to the forefront and researchers will find that there is an overall cosmic law which transcends all physical life here on Earth.

The researchers will also discover that as the survival energy disappears out of people's personal consciousness-related universe and everyday life, the function of the reptile brain will gradually evolve from representing the most basic and survival-related animal behaviour in the human body to instead becoming an instinctive-intuitive body energy – one that is able to sense and detect the basic structure of all spiritual and material energies, as well as the development possibilities which lie hidden in those energy structures.

You could say, that when the reptilian brain is lifted in frequency through body crystallisation and the subsequent activation of the Golden energy in the cells, miracles will happen in human behaviour. Aggression and adrenaline in the body will become linked with personal endurance instead of being used for going to battle.

Many other exciting discoveries will be made in the future. Thinking out of the box and outside the realm of the visible material reality and inside the spirit world will become the norm in the Golden Age, allowing us to get closer to the divine truth. Earth is not home to the divine creation and creative power without good reason! Moreover, thanks to the Golden energy, we humans cannot remain unaware of the great materialisation power that exists here on the planet. So if we think positively, we will continuously be allotted greater responsibility for spreading positivity to the outside world and if we think negatively, we will be deprived of the possibilities we have to influence other people, as negative thinking undermines their energy.

It is only when we humans have 'proved' to ourselves and to the Earth force that we can find balance within ourselves and with the people around us in our daily lives, that we will be able to activate the New Time Golden energy in our lives. So even though the Golden energy is down there, right under our feet, it is by no means public property.

We have to be deserving of accessing the New Time's powerful Golden energy by showing responsibility in everyday life and by being able to balance our own lives. The Crystal energy has definitely not been in vain. It is Crystal life-values and Crystal behaviour that are required of us humans, so that we can activate the Golden energy in a high frequency, powerful way in our lives.

No one can therefore claim that Earth's energy is unintelligent. It knows exactly how to influence and 'raise' people to become conscious, responsible citizens who want to help their fellow humans to also become responsible citizens and to achieve balance in life. If we humans do not do what is expected of us, in order that we can develop to become good, responsible citizens in the Golden Age, we will not get any opportunities to develop in our lives, and all the doors to success will be slammed right in our faces.

This is the Golden energy's very direct, specific and easily comprehensible way of showing us that if we do not contribute something to the Whole, we will not get anything back in return. This is how Earth's Golden energy interprets the concept of balance - no one can be in any doubt about who contributes to the Whole and who does not. Material resources will therefore be shuffled around a lot in the Golden Age, so acts of giving and receiving will be more attuned to each other than they are today.

Consequently, the Golden energy will initially reveal itself as the very accommodating, sympathetic, mediating and accepting party in any form of communication. However, if the need for balance is not respected by the other party, the energy may well give back in exactly the same way that people send out, so that they can better understand what is meant and also better understand their own behaviour.

Earth is not a naive planet which has invited various existences from out in the vast Cosmos to reside on the planet so that they can develop extraordinarily at Planet Earth's expense, while the planet looks on in silence.

Earth has its very own way of doing things and it often leaves it to life to teach people what they need to learn. This in no way excludes the possibility that you can learn by reading and listening to others but from 2013 it will be the school of life which will set the crucial agenda for what Earth's residents will learn in the future. The concept of 'consequence' is the result of getting involved in Earth's materialising powers because what you focus on and wish for is what you often get both on the positive and the negative level.

In the future, we humans will thus learn very much more about life and energies by digging even deeper down into matter than where we are now. When we learn from what is around us, Earth's overall knowledge level increases incrementally, even though it is not strictly the consciousness of Earth that is increasing but rather the consciousness of humanity.

WHEN THE CREATION ENERGY RAN AMOK

For many hundreds of thousands of years, Earth has been the nice one in the solar system, the planet who has opened the doors so that many entities from elsewhere could live, party and make use of the Golden spiritual materialisation power here on Planet Earth exactly as they wished. This happened in such places as Atlantis, Peru and Egypt, where the people and societies of that time were, in all likelihood, unable to handle the huge terrestrial materialisation power and dominion that Earth's energy had made available to them.

Those people and societies experienced, perhaps for the first time in the existence of their consciousness, that they were able to manifest physical and material things. It was so novel and exciting for them that they could not bring themselves to stop the process of creation, even though they had created everything that they needed. They continued to materialise and create objects and conditions which were further and further away from the spirit energy in the cosmic Source, with the result that they undermined their own existence.

If you are so greedy that you focus exclusively on materialising increasing amounts of condensed energy and physical objects around you, the spirit energy will finally disappear from your life – then you die. Spirit is eternal life, whereas matter is impermanent and therefore mortal, so you simply have a shorter life if you focus exclusively on the material energy in your life. People who are healthy and live a long time are often more implicated in their own spiritual and life impulses than with material energy.

Many alien beings around the Cosmos therefore concluded that Earth's energy was condensed, benighted and greedy and they decided to send assistance to Earth to help raise its frequency. However, *Earth* has *never* needed help – it is *us humans* who need help, we who have not been able to control our need to create and materialise, whether it applies to children, money or material objects.

Imagine if there had been no restrictions hampering our urge to create, so that we could earn all the money and have all the children we wanted. The planet would have been overpopulated a very long time ago, because the creation energy would have run amok... and who would then have taken care of collecting the rubbish, baking our bread and cleaning our homes if we all had the possibility of living like kings and queens? There would certainly not be many who would choose to be servants if they could be kings and queens instead... and with so many kings and queens everywhere on Earth, there would never be anyone to take care of these simple practical details of daily life, while the royals took care of their kingdoms. The material creation process would end up getting completely out of control, which would be limiting for all human and consciousness development on Earth and in maintaining the balance between people.

Chaos would ensue and it would not be the first time this has happened in the history of Planet Earth. This is exactly what has happened numerous times on Earth, where a number of highly developed societies have moved beyond the limit of what the creation energy could cope with regarding the maintaining of balance. When this limit is passed and a whole society is in full-throttle overdrive, creating all that it is possible to create on this Earth, then it will drive itself directly into the abyss. Things go belly-up and the restart button has to be pressed so that the creation process can begin all over again from scratch on the spirit level.

This happened on Atlantis, in Lemuria, Egypt, Peru and other places, where degeneration and decay set in and the spirit energy in a completely pure form – also known as death – came on the scene. Today, it is fortunately possible to integrate completely pure spirit energy into the body without dying, if you focus on creating balance between the spirit and the body instead of focusing only on one of the parts. Of course, this was not possible to the same extent in the aforementioned societies.

∞ ∞ ∞ ∞ ∞ ∞ ∞ ∞ ∞

Even though Earth's Golden energy is spiritually-materialising and creative in its basic structure, it has never had a focus on creating material objects without there being a need for them. The same has been the case for most indigenous peoples who have lived in different places on Earth.

Earth and its indigenous peoples, who in many cases were the first people on Earth in their respective lands and parts of the world, have instead focused on the spiritual life impulse which was a prerequisite for being able to survive and stay focused in the body. Consequently, they have, for example, often thanked the animals they have killed to enable themselves to survive for having made their body energy available in order that they could eat it and survive. One life has thus helped the other by renouncing its material body structure so that the other life could continue to live and maintain its material body structure.

Today, billions of animals are killed each year without being thanked for making their body energy available so that we humans can have something to eat. This is a very clear example of how the creation process in modern times does not significantly focus on the spiritual life impulse. Instead, it focuses on increasing its material energy by earning as much money as possible to create animal life that is predestined to die so that we humans can continue to live.

It is a fact that the more prevalent the material energy is in society, the less respect is given to the spiritual and life impulses in people and animals. Money is given precedence over human and animal life. This is not in keeping with the Golden energy's basic structure. Animal welfare will thus be a high priority in the Golden Age.

Earth's indigenous peoples, who originally had Golden spiritually-materialising energy within, without any energy-related influences from other planets, have rarely had the same need to surround themselves with material possessions as do the people who have come to Earth from the outside. People with extensive knowledge of Earth's energy know from experience that physical objects have no value in themselves but that the objects with which they surround themselves may have a historical value, due to the experiences that the objects remind them of. It is therefore the spirit in the physical objects that is important, together with the life experience and history which the objects represent. Objects can thus help people to be better at remembering their own history, so they can pass it on to their children and grandchildren. In this way, all sorts of buildings, monuments, paintings, machines and many other material objects throughout Earth's history have helped to provide clues to new generations about what happened earlier here on Planet Earth.

Focusing on creating material objects which can last for many generations to come thereby creates a historical, informative and educational effect which must be seen as being very positive.

Of course, there are still people on this Earth who focus exclusively on materialising objects from a selfish perspective but these people very often get acquainted with the opposite of the material, namely the spirit energy in its purest form. This often happens in connection with death or serious illness in the family or the like; situations which clearly show them that life cannot be bought with money. You can improve your quality of life with the help of money but money and material objects do not in themselves support vitality and love of life.

Love and vitality cannot be bought with money and the rent and our other bills cannot be paid with pure love. Consequently, all people on Earth are forced to deal with both love and money in physical life without these two having to act as each other's opposites. Establishing and maintaining the balance between spirituality, love, acceptance and being accommodating on the one hand and materialism and the ability to create forms and earn money on the other hand, is exactly what the creative Golden energy is about.

As a result, many people here on Earth often experience moving very deeply into Earth's dense material energy sphere when they feel love for another human being and the person they love is perceived almost as their physical property. These people obviously have to learn to distinguish between the energies that belong to their love relationship and those which belong to their material universe, something which Earth's Golden dualistic energy is a master at teaching them. In the Crystal energy and the Crystal-Golden and Golden energies, these two energies co-exist harmoniously. Jealousy and the idea of owning another human being simply do not exist.

THE GOOD AND THE BAD

Since the Golden energy began to stir inside Earth and now that it is also beginning to be activated at the cellular level in many crystallised human bodies – especially in children and adolescents as well as in a small group of adults – it is very difficult for it to keep quiet if there is something it is not satisfied with. This means, that in the future, we will see many more and larger-scale natural disasters and violent storms. The elements will, in many cases, show themselves from their rough-and-ready, not-so-nice sides, so that the air and earth can be cleansed of any negative energy and various high and low-frequency energies with which the Earth cannot reconcile itself.

Here on Planet Earth, from time immemorial, the intention has been that there has to be spiritual space and physical space so that many totally diverse energies can move around and co-exist. A prerequisite for this is that the respective energies keep the peace and show respect for one another, which unfortunately is not the case everywhere on the planet as I write. In many places, there continue to be wars between people, where one party sees itself as the light and its opponent as the darkness, a view which is reciprocated in the opposition camp. There is a tendency here on Earth to perceive what you do not like as dark and dirty, whereas you yourself are pure, bright and clean.

There is therefore a huge need to increase consciousness and insight in Earth's population as a whole, to be able to accommodate each other's differences and take care of the planet. Some people try to do this by using spirituality and spiritual science, while others approach the issue in a more concrete and down-to-earth manner that can be both seen and felt. What these two groups have in common is that they both have positive intentions but they do not understand each other at all. That is precisely what Earth's Golden energy wants to change by all possible means.

The Golden energy is therefore happy to send a violent hurricane to destroy people's houses, so that they have to learn to get support from one another and have something to share. It also has no trouble pressurising extremely spiritual people out onto the established labour market to earn some money, so they are forced to mix with 'ordinary' people, because that will help them to create new, different relationships which can expand their consciousness in many different directions. Extremely well-off people can also experience losing everything they own, so that they have to learn to understand that you can have a good life and be happy even if you have no money.

Everything is possible when the Golden energy is part of the decision-making process. Consequently, most people should be happy that the Crystal energy was responsible for leading the overall consciousness development on Earth before the Golden energy broke through to the surface. The Crystal energy took part in the process of decision-making regarding exactly how cooperation is going to work here on Earth in the future, so it still has a lot to say. Therefore, in the future, when the Golden energy has behaved like a bit of a 'bad guy' because it is in a hurry and therefore often chooses quick and sometimes violent solutions because there are so many imbalances that need to be rectified, the Crystal energy will come in as the 'good guy' to ensure that balance is present on all levels.

That is why the Crystal-Golden energy (and the balance between the two) must find its way into the body so that the Golden energy cannot just take full control of the human body. This will never happen, because in Earth's interior, there is a merging process in which the integration of opposing energies takes place. This is similar to the one that is taking place in every human on the surface of Planet Earth. Another reason that the Crystal energy has preceded the Golden energy is that the Crystal and Golden energies, combined in their highest potency, represent the Diamond energy that will be activated in all new-born children's bodies before the end of this century.

The merging of the Crystal and the Golden energies would not have been possible, however, if the Golden energy had preceded the Crystal energy and had been in charge of the process alone. It just cannot keep still for as long as it takes to compress pure Diamond energy in the human body and especially not if there are a lot of interesting things going on around it! There is no doubt whatsoever that people with Golden energy are attracted to the Diamond energy but most of all to diamonds in their physical form.

In Earth's interior alone, it takes millions of years to create Diamond energy in its physical form and the process takes place at a leisurely pace deep down within Planet Earth, free of external influences and distractions that would otherwise shift the focus from this unique process of creation. Now, however, the Diamond energy in human form is in sight but it is taking an extremely long time to be created, if we compare it with the average lifespan of most humans. However, the Diamond energy is being brought into the human energy structure from one life to the next, in the same way as the Crystal energy and the Golden energy have been, so we cannot really compare the Diamond compression process in humans with the way Earth creates natural diamonds. After all, they stay in the same place and on the same frequency for millions of years, which we humans do not!

∞ ∞ ∞ ∞ ∞ ∞ ∞ ∞ ∞

The Golden energy largely follows its own inner impulse and is not always tolerant if people or energies from outside try to interfere, not even if the energies come here from our solar system or from other places outside the solar system. They will pretty much be sent home again with a kick up the backside, because the Golden energy is not afraid to state clearly what it thinks about things. Maybe it is a good thing that it has remained hidden deep inside Earth and all the way down on the cellular level in the human body until now!

If you sometimes wonder why there are storms in your area again, or why the air around you seems charged and almost electric, then it is probably because Earth is in the process of cleaning up close to where you live. It may also be because the frequencies in your neighbourhood are part of other contexts in Earth's energy and they are affected when the energies in a completely different place on Planet Earth are being worked on, because the Golden energy is working night and day to get everything under control. This means, among other things, that if many people with a certain nationality are living in another country and there is unrest in their homeland, it will also affect the balance, the weather and the energies of the country in which they live.

Maybe you even experience that your sleep is being affected because it feels like there is a light switched on in the bedroom all night. If that is the case, you are being kept awake by the light but also by the hum of Earth's Golden energy, which may well be vacuuming and working all night on the consciousness level to be ready for the next morning. A huge clean-up is actually happening on Earth's inner levels, of which we have seen but a very small part of as yet but all life on Earth's surface is affected by it.

The Golden energy is fighting with both friends and enemies to get them to take their rightful place, where they will interfere neither with one another nor with the overall balance here on Planet Earth. Kindly-disposed spiritual beings from other realms are therefore being sent back in their droves to their own galaxies at the very moment they come here wanting to help Earth on the conscious level.

Many entities and spiritual beings who have been held captive in Earth's interior for thousands or hundreds of thousands of years, either because they have not had the strength and insight to escape, or because they have been so unbalanced in their energy that their home planet did not want to have them back, are now being sent back to the places they originally came from. The extent of the clean-up work going on in Earth's interior is something we people living on the surface in the visible world cannot possibly begin to imagine.

When this both fundamental and comprehensive clean-up work is completed at some time in the future, many imbalances will disappear from the surface of Earth. For example, there will no longer be a need for people to take euphoriants to induce hallucinations and strong psychic, ecstatic and/or conscious-ness-expanding experiences in the brain. When the clean-up has taken place in the frequencies and energy layers in Earth's interior which correspond to the frequencies of the brain that need euphoriant and hallucinogenic drugs to connect to certain dream-like, nightmarish and/or horror and anxiety-provoking impulses, the brain's need for drugs disappears. The Golden energy in the body will then be able to help promote various positive impulses in the brain itself simply by focusing on them.

MAINTAIN THE BALANCE

Imagine that you take a large, luscious African woman who is good at dancing and wiggling her backside and who has really good rhythm in her body and is happy with it, no matter how it looks. Then you take a Nordic woman who has a slightly chilly, distant and balanced manner and is in control of everything in life including her goals and priorities, as well as her personal radiance and weight – and then you meld these two women together. What you will then have is exactly the energy constellation which many men and women everywhere on Earth experience in their bodies when they are fully crystallised and then begin activating the Golden energy at the cellular level.

The Golden energy loves dancing, partying, living life to the full and being sociable whereas the Crystal energy focuses on constantly setting new goals in life and creating overview and balance, as well as taking responsibility for itself and its surroundings. In other words, you can say that the Golden energy has a constant focus on expanding and breaking all boundaries – including weight – and freeing itself completely from all responsibility, while the Crystal energy tries to bring balance to life and to the body.

The Golden energy is your best friend and the one you love the most but if the Crystal energy does not settle in your energy system first, so it can help your Golden energy to be constructive and goal-oriented, you risk getting far too much uncontrollable terrestrial creation power activated in your body. This is a power that is hard to stop and correspondingly hard to control... and this power can cause you to forget important things, or you will not get round to them on time because your own spontaneous actions are interfering with your planning.

It is obviously not possible that you will be permitted to use all your vitality in partying and having fun and redefining norms, just because you feel like it. Redefining norms and established frameworks was what the Indigo energy was about and it almost killed the older generation! Most people party in an irresponsible way when they are young, so that is a phase most adults have been through. Consequently, there have to be other solutions for adults to be able to maintain their youthful life impulse in a responsible way without doing stupid things. This is where the Crystal energy steps in.

So always focus first on giving space to the responsible and balanced Crystal energy in whatever you are doing by planning or creating an overview of the situation for yourself. Otherwise, you risk the Golden creation energy taking over completely so you lose control. Also pay attention to the fact that you have only been given the opportunity to live a life here on Planet Earth because you have a life mission and/or something to learn.

If you have a life mission on the spirit level, then the Crystal energy in your body will guide you to put your life task and your dharma into practice. You have yourself played a part in agreeing your dharma before you were born and you have your own free will to choose in which direction and in what way you want to realise your dharma. However, you will not get the opportunity to leave this planet before it is completed.

If, however, you have a life task on the soul level, it is a part of your karma and pre-determined destiny, meaning that your life is planned and already set up down to the smallest detail. Your karma often relates to something that you need to learn in life and once you have learned it, you have the option of upgrading your consciousness to the spirit level by, for example, having an AuraTransformation™. This means that your aura will be upgraded from the soul level to the Crystal level, so that you can begin to get to grips with your dharma and spiritual life mission, which is stored at the cellular level in your body. Here, the Golden energy will be extremely helpful in enabling you to enjoy life, when you have at some point completed the crystallisation in your body, as it makes living your dharma truly enjoyable, along with those things that you have been born to do and that you have accepted to do before you were born.

Briefly, an AuraTransformation™ makes you karma-free because karma is the link to the astral body, (also called the emotional body) in the soul aura which dissolves during AuraTransformation™. It is therefore possible for people to become karma-free when they let go of their own astral body and therefore leave the soul level. It does not necessarily have to be the product of an AuraTransformation™.

For example, if you lose your soul aura following a shock or a near-death experience, you will also be karma-free but you will have no protection in the aura quite simply because it has been dissolved. This means that external energies and impressions will have direct access to your physical body because you no longer have a private, protective zone around your body to keep away other people's energies. This can be likened to living in a house with neither outside walls nor roof, so anyone can drop by and settle down on the comfortable sofa, for as long as they like.

You can of course throw them out of your house but if they refuse to leave, you will have to fight permanently against the intrusion as you no longer have energetic protection from the world around you and therefore cannot lock the doors. Consequently, you will not sleep as well at night as you could because you must constantly be on guard in case someone tries to creep into your energy. You may well sleep but your intuition will be working overtime and will risk burn-out. You could also become allergic to anything that comes in from the outside because eventually, you may be unable to distinguish between your friends and your enemies. The same applies to the food you eat.

When you have an AuraTransformation™, you can still have a lot of memories stored in your body from your upbringing and from past lives on the soul level. These bodily memories are tied up in various parts of the body and can feel like karma. They often seem almost predestined in their energy structure, because they can help to keep you in certain behaviour patterns and habits and they are only released when you have completed the body crystallisation process. Crystallisation of the body has nothing to do with your AuraTransformation™ but crystallisation of the body is initiated on its own after the AuraTransformation™, because you feel extra-protected from the outside world and therefore can begin to focus very deeply on the development of your own consciousness.

Many spiritual people often have fewer negative bodily memories than non-spiritual people because they are not familiar with terrestrial energy and the way in which a human body can function. Consequently, many spiritual people have not stored so many negative experiences at the cellular level, simply because they have not been able to relate to either the experience or to their own bodies. If you have many negative bodily memories, it is usually a sign that you have lived many lives on the soul level here on Earth which you need to have processed and cleaned up so you can get on with living your life on the spirit level.

On the one hand, spiritual people may not have a tendency to collect negative bodily memories. On the other hand, they often have great resistance to occupying their physical bodies, which may result in different kinds of blockages in the body that are often mental in nature. This is because they use their mental will to try to control what is happening in their body and therefore, the natural state of flow disappears.

An AuraTransformation™ can often contribute to very spiritual people starting to feel comfortable in their own bodies but the feeling of well-being only usually remains if they have a personal desire to start living a terrestrial life in harmony with people who are different from themselves. If they only want to mix with people who are exactly like themselves, there is no point at all in them upgrading the aura to the spirit level.

OPPOSITES MEET

The Golden energy is the optimal 'add-on' to the goal-oriented and balance-focused Crystal energy. It makes working towards achieving your goals in life and doing what you were born to do pleasurable and exciting rather than humdrum and banal.

The Golden energy makes you extra-committed and productive, as well as creative and cheerful. It spreads a lot of joy when it feels inspired. It therefore also enables you motivate those around you to make a huge positive difference in many, many ways.

If the Golden energy is strongly present in a group of people, many fundamental disagreements can be accepted, as long as the parties involved show respect and acceptance in relation to one another. The Golden energy never tries to provoke or pressurise other people to think differently from what feels right for them.

In the Golden Age, we will, figuratively speaking, live almost like animals on the savannah. This means balance all around and everyone being well fed and satisfied with life and consequently, everyone will be able walk the streets freely without being bothered or harassed by others. However, when it is 'feeding time' for the group of people who are low frequency in their energy and have little money, more primal characteristics will come to the fore in those people. Then, the more sensitive people will have to be careful not to move out into the open where they are visible to everyone, because they will risk their personal energy being eaten by these 'energy predators'.

In a terrestrial context, you should therefore be extra-conscious about where you are and who you choose to spend your time with, not only on the physical level but even more importantly, on the energetic level. The difference between then and now consists in the fact that the spiritual energy will fill more and more of physical human consciousness and the physical element will occupy more and more of the consciousness of spiritual people. The two worlds thus begin to come together into one and the same world. People will gradually begin to perceive the part that was previously totally alien to them in a more concrete and attentive way.

This means that all contradictions which fundamentally have the same energetic source, but which express themselves in the opposite way to each other, start to combine. This applies not only to dichotomies in society but also within each person in the form of, for example, light and darkness. Both sides of us humans begin to appear simultaneously, even though most people on the soul level often see just one side at a time. So when you see one side with your physical eyes, you cannot avoid sensing and registering the other side with your other senses. This combination enables you to have access to good overall insight regarding others.

In the Golden Age, we humans need both light and dark and rest and activity to keep us alive and vital. If we do not get the opportunity to rest and recharge and we are always on red alert on the level of our energy systems, without allowing space for the dark which surrounds us when we sleep, our energy will soon run out because our brains become stressed. The brain needs to surround itself with the darkness in order to be able to balance itself and recharge.

In the Golden energy, there is no room for pretending that people, situations and objects have a meaning for us which they do not have. Therefore, in many ways, it is so much easier to be a human being because we no longer have to pretend that things are different from how they really are. However, a lot of time will be spent creating or experiencing the unique taste, smell or sound, the unique emotional experience as well as travel experience, etc., which is often achieved by combining things that do not at first appear to go together. The Golden energy is also about creating both entirely new ways of working and entirely new realities, as well as creating your own life by combining the best of the different worlds and universes that you personally comprehend.

This means that you need to focus on living out your own inner creative power, which in its deepest essence, is a mix of high-frequency spiritual energy and materially condensed energy, without you becoming a rather poor copy of someone else.

Create your own outer reality and identity based on who you really are deep down inside. Always ensure that you maintain balance in your own life and in the things that you choose to include in your life. By doing this, you will ensure that not much can go wrong for you.

USE WHAT YOU HAVE LEARNED

Looking at where consciousness development has led us to today, it initially seems that many spiritual people are at a stage in their consciousness development where they have to pay additional attention to their bodies and the balance in their bodies in order to survive. Many people have thus been obliged to focus on diet, health and exercise, even though they may never before have had a desire to focus so much on the physical framework of life to which the body belongs.

The importance of our bodies being in balance during this period cannot be over-emphasised. Without this balance, there is a great risk that your physical body will not be able to handle the large amounts of high-frequency energy and consciousness which, both now and in the future, will be finding their way into the most material and condensed part of us, namely, our bodies.

If our bodies were not able to cope with the new high-frequency energies, they would not be able to keep up with the consciousness development either and then we could be in a very grave situation as human beings. Our bodies are tools and our means of expression in the physical world. If we were not able to express ourselves through our bodies, then we would be totally invisible to most people! This means, among other things, that we would not be able to realise the things in life that are important to us. So the body can in many ways be likened to our materialisation ability that enables us to change our lives and the world around us if it is strong and well-developed.

What is the use of a strong body without a strong aura?

It is absolutely no coincidence that many spiritual people choose to focus on strengthening and upgrading their auras before they begin to upgrade their body energy, because they would not get far in the physical world with a leaky aura - taking care of their own energy would be a round the clock job, in order to ensure that they are not being invaded by other people's energies. You can read about this in the earlier chapter *Maintain The Balance.*

Many spiritual people often think that they have to continue digging in their consciousness to find even more blockages and experiences from their childhoods and past lives that they have to let go of in order to raise their consciousness frequency. As a result, they continue, in therapy, to dig even deeper into the system and get a grip on what lies furthest within themselves. At some point, however, it may be appropriate for them to stop and look clearly at what it really is that they are doing, because, to be perfectly honest, you cannot continue to dig deeper if you want to feel joy in your physical life here on Earth and have time to live it to the full.

The extent of the deep insights that many spiritual people 'find' is often not commensurate with the consciousness dividends they receive from digging deeper. Therefore it is essential to be able to draw the line and say "I have learned enough for this time. Instead, I now need to use the things I have learned and understood in my life to live life and help others, otherwise I will end up being an eternal spiritual student, who never proves to myself or to others that I can use the things I have learned in my life for something constructive which will benefit both myself and the Whole."

Therapy is, of course, useful if you have something weighing you down and you know within yourself that there is more for you to learn on the personal level if you take that route. When, however, you have worked intensively for several years to get in touch with the deeper layers of yourself, you have let go of everything you can and you feel that you have achieved balance within in yourself and your life, then it is time to adjust your perspective on life. Among the many contradictions that you will experience having to combine in life, will be your past and your present, which you should try to balance in the best way you can. It is no use just focusing either on the past or on the future. Live in the now and try from there to combine your past and your present, so that you achieve personal balance and joy in your life.

On our way from childhood to adulthood, we all go through the 'school of life' to learn about life on Planet Earth and about ourselves. We then put our learning into practice for the benefit of ourselves and of others while we are alive. So make sure that you 'walk the talk' and do what you say you will, because then you will be the best role model for others and your joy of living will automatically increase. It is important, however, that you first discover what your personal truth is, because otherwise it will be hard for you to put it into practice.

It is so easy to copy other people and there are so many people to copy who have different and perhaps better ways of doing things than you. However, if the copied and learned behaviour does not basically match your personality, other people will always get a feeling that you are not completely true to yourself and therefore not true to them either. You will then understand that it is really not advantageous for you to 'photocopy' the energy and behaviour of others.

Always search inside yourself to find out what you think about life and about other people. Feel how you react, in different parts of your body, to various experiences, people and situations. You will slowly begin to get an idea of who you are and what you and your body think about things. The answer to this should be found not only in your heart or your brain but in the whole of your body.

Choose your role models wisely and find your own inspiration instead of copying everything you see and hear just because it seems more interesting than what you do, know and stand for as a human being right now. There is always someone who needs to hear your precise truth.

If you think your life is hard, and you have had a difficult childhood, that it is hard for you to leave your self-pity behind, do something good for others instead of sitting at home feeling sorry for yourself. Then your life will begin to make more sense. Life is to be lived and all of us go through our own individual consciousness expansion processes, which cannot be compared to other people. Everything is individual and everything is experienced differently by everyone. So do yourself a favour and take action to do something good to help others. In so doing, you will not have time to feel your own pain. However, if you have lost someone close, you will need time to regain your personal balance.

Please note that you cannot always help other people. Especially if they have not even realised that they need help or they cannot see the extent of their own problems. There is no reason, either, to feel sorry for people who do not even understand that they have problems. Instead, help those who want to improve their personal situations and who are willing to accept your help with open arms. It will bring joy to both your life and theirs.

THE BIRTH OF THE GOLDEN ENERGY

According to the majority of the many experts all over the world who have studied the Mayan calendar attentively, Earth's Golden energy was activated on 21 December 2012. This did not mean that an explosive conversion of the physical energy took place across Earth on that date. Even though the Golden energy is very spontaneous and lively, it is now working on an equal footing with the Crystal energy, which has its main focus on love-intelligence, balance, responsibility and overview. This is because it would not be advantageous to suddenly make available an ultra-powerful spiritual materialisation power that the people of today have never known and therefore would not have an earthly chance of being able to handle in a balanced way.

As a result, the Golden energy will gradually be released on an on-going basis into everyone's body awareness as the years go by, as each individual becomes able to manage the energy in a balanced way. Thus 21 December 2012 represents the day the Earth's interior power was born into the New Time and began making itself visible on Earth's surface.

Fortunately, there are very few new bosses who start extensive restructuring and big changes on the very first day in a new job, where they do not yet have personal experience of how things work in the new company. So it would be naive to think that Earth's energy would turn everything upside down on the very first day that it is visible. However, we can look forward to fundamental changes taking place at a much faster rate than before in the way that we relate to life – especially if we are aware of the current energy shift between the pure Crystal energy and the Crystal-Golden energy.

There will be an extra-strong focus on all forms of growth and many exciting new inventions that far surpass the present human imagination will see the light of day. This will happen because the Golden energy, due to its great insight into how life energy and the creative power function in all contexts, can help to create growth and save lives in completely new ways. It will therefore be very interesting to see what the combination of knowledge from Earth's interior, along with that of our solar system and other planets, solar systems and galaxies around the Cosmos, may result in when the creative Golden energy really starts to show what it can do.

However, people on Earth should be prepared to handle these new inventions and extraordinary opportunities in a responsible manner, so that they get the chance to be created in the first place. This is because the Crystal energy does not permit innovations which risk being abused because of people's lack of insight and ignorance. If that also includes a desire to gain power, influence and enormous financial gains through such inventions, without the Whole simultaneously being taken into account, permission for the realisation of the inventions will not be granted, regardless of where these negative intentions come from.

Very creative people can thus find themselves experiencing significant delays and problems associated with their creative processes if it is not the right time for a particular idea or new product to be marketed. There are many financial string-pullers, hackers, copy cats, idea stealers and the like, all over Earth, who will be obliged to have their personal consciousness upgraded so that future inventions and progress can find their way into society without being abused, manipulated or exposed to financial speculation.

LIFE TASKS VERSUS CONSCIOUSNESS LEVEL IN THE NEW TIME

All Indigo people have a transformation task that they were born to carry out. Consequently, many of them were born with a disproportionately small amount of the Water element in their personal energy although they do have lots of Fire, Earth and Air.

When you do not have much Water, you do not generally prioritise personal qualities such as intuition, empathy and adaptability in relation to those around you, making it possible for Indigo people to just forge ahead without consideration for others if there is something they are really enthusiastic about getting done.

They imagine, of course, that they are taking the Whole into account in everything they do but they often do not like the methods that other people may use. Therefore, they have no problem with turning everything upside down, so that imbalances emerge and become visible, in order for balance to be restored.

This is because tracking any imbalances and then correcting them is a part of Indigo people's overall life tasks. The more visibility they manage to give to any unbalanced situations, the better. High visibility is required to spread a message to many people simultaneously and in terms of visibility, all Indigo people are right at home. They love being seen and heard!

Indigos are often very visible regarding the digestion process - both literally and metaphorically. If they do not like a certain food, or if it does not really agree with them, you will certainly know about it! They are generally very sensitive in their energy systems and they do not really have this under control, so when taking in either food or experiences, there are often allergic reactions on both the physical or human levels.

Nothing happens discreetly when Indigos are involved. However, they often respond extremely quickly to balancing and alternative treatments, as well as food supplements and a healthy diet. They do not generally feel attracted to traditional Western medicine.

∞ ∞ ∞ ∞ ∞ ∞ ∞ ∞ ∞

When both Indigo youngsters and adults begin crystallising in their bodies, they often change their personal behaviour. Their underlying energy may still be just as provocative and rebellious as it always was, and perhaps they will still have a few transformation tasks which they will have to bring about, but they do start, to a much greater extent than before, to adapt to their environment. They also begin very visibly making space for other people in their lives. They often simply choose to cooperate with others because they are now in the process of integrating more Water into their consciousness. They therefore start taking more notice of other people, as Water is the most sociable element of the four. Moreover, they no longer need to be the centre of attention all the time.

Those Indigos born with a pure Indigo aura in the period from 1995 until around 2004, and the adults who have had an Aura-Transformation™, do not simply crystallise in their bodies. They also crystallise in their auras and in their network energy. At some point they become Crystal people instead of Indigo people, with their main focus being on balance in their lives.

Adults with Indigo energy who have not had their auras transformed and are therefore still on the soul level will not be able to crystallise in their auras. They will therefore often continue to provoke their environment due to their particular radiance, which unfortunately is not fully in harmony with their body energy if the body has already crystallised. This means that other people often do not like their radiance, as it does not match their body energy.

Those around them, however, do not feel antagonised by their physical actions if the body is crystallised, because they often do all the right things. Others just cannot stand being close to them but they cannot explain why. So, people with Indigo energy on the soul level, who do *not* have an Indigo aura, are definitely not the most popular people on Planet Earth.

∞ ∞ ∞ ∞ ∞ ∞ ∞ ∞ ∞

Crystal people are rarely as uncontrollably hypersensitive regarding food and the environment as Indigos. Crystal people are very sensitive but as they often know what they are getting into before they have even left the house to go out, they are not likely to get surprised in the same way as Indigos, who are often completely unprepared for what awaits them.

'Crystals' are extremely skilled at preventing and preparing for the many different situations in life that they have often chosen for themselves. If there is something they do not want to do, they will not do it unless there are very strong arguments in favour of doing it. Even though they are extremely sensitive, they have a very strong psyche and are fully balanced in their basic energies. It therefore takes a lot to knock them off their stride, even when the going gets really tough. They are also extremely good at balancing themselves both physically and energetically if they have been pushing themselves too hard for a while.

Crystals are often very particular and conscious both about

what they eat and who they want to spend time with. They are selective to such an extent that they can often say no to food and experiences because there are energies around with which they cannot fully identify. Consequently, they will not be able to bring themselves to eat food prepared by a chef who has had a bad day. They will keep well away from any places where the energy is not at its best and may choose to return to the restaurant on another day when the energy feels better. Crystals are masters at reading other people's energies as well as those in the environment – even at a distance. They will not therefore go out somewhere, only to turn back and go elsewhere. On the other hand, they have no problem eating food that is not normally a part of their diet if it feels good. Generally, though, they are very aware of what they are taking in on all levels in their daily lives.

Even though all Crystals (children and adults with Crystal energy in their auras) represent balance, they never force their personal balance energy and knowledge down the throats of others, even though the spreading of balance and insight are among their most important life tasks. They would rather keep away if they sense that those around them are not looking for balance. This is because Crystals want to transform and balance the world on a 'volunteer' basis, so they are always looking for the places where the willingness to acquire new knowledge, to change and be in balance are greatest.

Many Indigos who spontaneously upgrade the energy in their auras from Indigo to Crystal, and who also have Crystal bodies and a fully crystallised network energy, begin to behave like pure Crystals due to their energy upgrades if they have life tasks on the Crystal level. However, if they have life tasks in the Crystal-Golden energy, they will also have to activate the Golden energy on the cellular level in the body.

∞ ∞ ∞ ∞ ∞ ∞ ∞ ∞ ∞

Those with Crystal auras and Crystal-Golden energy integrated and activated in their bodies are more relaxed and easy-going than Indigos and pure Crystals. This is because they truly embody the Earth pulse and life force, so they are ready to live life to the full, while taking responsibility for both their own development and that of others. They know, both intuitively and instinctively, what is good for people, animals and for the planet as a whole. They are generally involved in many positive initiatives that benefit the Whole as part of their Crystal-Golden life tasks – often without consulting with others.

Crystal-Golden people's life tasks often include social and humanitarian aspects.

All new initiatives and changes are carried out in a simple, straightforward way and Crystal-Golden people never feel excluded if they are the only ones eating a certain type of food, dressing in a certain way or having certain opinions. They rarely talk about what they do and why they do it. In fact, it is the great joy of being radiating from their bodies into their auras, as well as their deep, inner peace, which makes other people want to be like them, follow them and do as they do. Crystal-Golden people with Crystal auras are walking advertisements for any lifestyle they feel comfortable with. Almost all of them travel in different directions in life because they have different life purposes. On the other hand, they are very sociable, enjoy being in the company of many different types of people and are hungry for knowledge about many different topics.

They have well-developed memories and memory is distributed over all the body's various intelligences, not just the brain. They stock their thoughts and observations just as well with their stomach, feet and necks but, of course, these parts of the body remember in a different way from the brain.

Their strong Golden life force and deep insight into life, combined with the Crystal balance in their bodies, make many people want to change spontaneously when they have been close to Crystal-Golden people. Fortunately, Crystal-Golden people have a strong sense of responsibility in all contexts, which means that they do not want to influence others for their own personal gain, which in turn means that other people will always feel safe around them.

It is not possible for people with a soul aura and Crystal-Golden energy in the body to balance as well in life. They will often alternate between being very proactive, initiating then over-adaptable and resigned regarding their respective life destinies, which they cannot change, unless they have had a Crystal aura upgrade.

Talking about how people with pure, high-frequency upgraded Golden energy in the body put their dharma into practice, regardless of whether they have a soul aura, an Indigo aura or a Crystal aura, makes no sense whatsoever, because this is never going to happen. The next step in the development of human consciousness after the Crystal and the Crystal-Golden body energy is actually the Diamond energy, which is extremely pure, sharp and multi-faceted in its personal expression. This means that the Diamond people of the future will look at themselves and life from many different angles, while they will consist of several different consciousnesses combined into one and the same body. This is possible because in their past lives they have lived in several different bodies simultaneously, which will all cooperate in the future and be one identical energy in one body. This is something they will be very conscious of and which will mean that they will be able to influence those around them in many different ways just by being close to them.

No one here on Earth has pure Diamond energy, as yet, in their body consciousness.

WHAT WILL BE POSSIBLE IN THE FUTURE?

Many spiritual people are extremely interested in knowing whether we will be able to communicate directly with other people and higher consciousnesses out in the universe when Earth increases in frequency. The truth is that we have always been able to communicate with other consciousnesses. However, this has been happening through people's physical bodies, because everyone has the imprint of different external consciousnesses in their individual body cell memory. In fact, we only need to take a quick look out over Earth and we can easily spot many people with energy structures and spiritual insights that are different from our own.

Here on Earth, we will not be communicating directly with external consciousnesses on the physical plane until far into the Diamond Age. At that point in time, the human body will be so strong that it will be able to hold itself together, regardless of which consciousness-related and consciousness-expanding influences it is exposed to. This is definitely not the case today, when people around Planet Earth would be traumatised if they saw external consciousnesses on the physical level as they truly look in their places of origin. This is because many external high-frequency energies cannot be converted to a visible, spiritual-material, terrestrial energy as long as there is still soul energy on this planet. It is not possible at the moment, even on the Crystal level, to make these external high-frequency energies appear as they really are, so that people can relate to them whilst awake on the everyday consciousness level.

In the Diamond Age, we will be able to detect different forms of life in space when we travel to other planets that have a different structure of consciousness from the spiritual-material energy we know from Earth. Today, it is possible to land on another planet or on the Moon when we go there in our terrestrial spacecraft but we are not yet able to see with our own eyes the real life on the planet with our terrestrial consciousness. On the other hand, we are capable, as modern conscious people and through our mental imagination, of moving our consciousness to certain specific frequencies where we can register different external energies and experiences, depending on where we are in life with our own consciousness.

It will also not be until the Diamond Age that the human body will be able to heal itself using a cell regeneration system that scientists will discover in the DNA structure of human stem cells. If using healthy stem cells in a human cannot help to prevent a particular disease from spreading or a body from degenerating, then in some cases, stem cells will be taken from other people who are almost identical in their body structure to that person, just as blood is donated today to people with the same blood type. This method will also mean that people in the future will be able to develop body consciousness; it will also be used for changing the behaviour of people who cannot find balance in their own bodies and minds. First and foremost, however, the method will be used to correct physical disabilities in people who are in pain or who are limited in their physical development because of body misalignments or similar.

The aforementioned cell regeneration system will be discovered while Earth is still in the Crystal-Golden Age, where it will initially be used to prevent environmental pollution and curb global warming, which will wreak havoc in the coming decades.

Regarding the degradation of various types of environmental pollution, it will be possible in many cases to drive pollution from everywhere on Earth back to its physical source, in the same way as will happen one day to the Cosmos, after which a new Big Bang will take place. The degradation will partly occur due to us being able to bio-degrade all the particles and frequencies that are part of the contaminated material by their frequency-related antipole and thereby neutralising a lot of the pollution. However, there is never any justification for pollution; so in the Crystal-Golden Age, many people will work intensively to discover even more environmentally friendly and healthy solutions than those found in industry today.

In the Crystal-Golden Age, from 2040, there will no longer be 'fate' in the same way as there was on the soul level until 1995. By that time, most people with soul energy will be retired and the Crystal energy will have prevailed in society for more than twenty years, starting with the current Crystal children entering the job market.

From that point in time, all adults will follow their inner impulses, which exist at the cellular level in the body and it will feel totally wrong for them not to do so. If they do not listen to their own bodies, it will mean that they are not listening to their own energies and they will lose their foothold in life. Following your dharma does not mean that you do not have any influence on your life. All Crystal people make it a major priority to do their very best for society and for Earth. They still have free will to live their lives as they wish, as long as they fulfil their life tasks, which, incidentally, they agreed to before they were born. It is precisely their dharma which determines how their body consciousness is put together at the human level.

Consequently, everyone will be precisely as they are because it is part of their life task to either be sensitive and understanding or else very specific and direct in their approach to this world. For example, a surgeon who bursts into tears every time he operates on a patient because he can feel the emotional processes through which the patient is going strongly in his own body, would not be much use!

∞ ∞ ∞ ∞ ∞ ∞ ∞ ∞ ∞

At the time of writing *(December 2014)*, most modern societies around the world are in the process of transition between the Indigo and the Crystal periods. This is because all the young people who have entered the job market in recent years have Indigo and Crystal auras and this naturally affects the overall business and economic development in society. Young people are always more energy-updated than the older generation, although this does not mean that they have greater experience at work than the older generation.

It means, rather, that they are a part of setting the energy agenda for how society will evolve in the future when they get older and gain more direct influence in different sorts of companies, governments and so on, all around the world.

In the current Indigo and Crystal period, many different new inventions and imitations are appearing everywhere on Earth. Many new methods of treatment, as well as various slimming and accounting systems and many different machines for home and leisure and a lot more besides, are being introduced all over the world, so we really need to be able to distinguish between what works and what does not. Many of these new inventions were not created by people with high-frequency Crystal energy or Crystal-Golden energy integrated and activated in their bodies. Rather, they are the creations of fortune hunters on the soul level and in some cases on the Indigo level, who are copying other people's products and methods. In many cases, test results will also be tampered with in order to get more customers, but because the majority of the Indigo energy will not accept that, the people concerned will be exposed as liars.

Many young Indigos are very interested in their appearance and personal image, especially when it comes to skin care, clothing, computers, mobiles and so on and they will not accept being cheated. As a result, dishonest companies will be 'outed' on the Internet and in the media if they do not have the best practice. We can currently see this trend spreading like wildfire among young people. Never cheat a young Indigo person if you are hoping to run a successful business for many years to come! In such cases, the judicial authorities will not even need to get involved, because thanks to the Indigos, society itself judges the companies in question by exerting a massive influence on other young people via social media.

Social media also help to market a lot of good products and positive initiatives, without the vendors having to pay for advertising. Good products sell all by themselves in Indigo Land.

In the Crystal period, which will increasingly gain ground out in the world community in the period from 2020 until 2040, there will be far more focus on creating products based on responsibility, respect and balance, which are of benefit to nature and will not damage it. In fact, this trend will even spread to small communities around the world where you would not immediately expect people to have a Crystal focus.

This will happen because all parents the world over will quite naturally be influenced by their Crystal children and Crystal-Golden children; so although the parents may not have Crystal auras, they will choose to live and eat healthily and also to exercise. In this way, the body will begin to spontaneously crystallise and those parents will naturally do something good for the world, even though it was not necessarily their original intention.

WHAT WILL CHILDREN AND ADULTS OF THE FUTURE BE LIKE?

Everyone in the future, regardless of whether they are Crystal, Crystal-Golden or Diamond in their energy, will think both holistically and individually. This is a future trend that will spread further out into the three aforementioned consciousness types' networks around the world community, especially to areas where many children live, because they will help to support this way of thinking at the consciousness level. Whenever possible, the three types of consciousness will try to participate as a fully integrated part of any whole they are a part of, whether it is at work or in private, while always maintaining their personal integrity.

Indigo people will also think holistically but mostly of their own personal wholeness and after that any 'wholes' that may interest them personally.

In society, development will usually take place at a much slower pace than is the case with individual personal development, since at a societal level, many very different types of people and levels of consciousness always have to be taken into account simultaneously. It is a very large and very time-consuming task for Earth's creation and creative power and for the Venus-Crystal love-intelligence, to bring the terrestrial cabal into alignment quickly and in a balanced way and it is the balancing itself that is the problem. Many people who find themselves on the soul level do not actually know what balance is if it is not included as an important element in their karma and destiny in their present life.

As I have already said in my book "Balance on All Levels with the Crystal and Indigo Energies", Crystal adults of the future will be very aware of how they raise and influence their children in daily life. They have a great feeling of responsibility and they will be very direct and straightforward when bringing up their children. They will start by making great demands on their children even when they are only small and curious, after which a more creative, thoughtful way of bringing up children will be put in place to inspire them to learn more. If the parents have Crystal-Golden energy, creative and abstract thinking will be prioritised more during childhood and adolescence.

The same approach will be used in schools and day-care centres worldwide to ensure that each child's ethical, compassionate and academic foundation is stable enough to be built safely upon.

All Crystal children need a good, stable base in life so that they can develop positively and if it is not possible to give them this, it is very important that they are given an explanation as to why this is not possible. This is because they need to understand the connections between everything so that they can better set up their own personal consciousness to cope with the various challenges in their lives.

Crystal-Golden children are better at coping with challenges than Crystal children but they do need regular rest so that they can recharge their bodies, otherwise their reserves will rapidly dry up. The old virtues of peace, cleanliness and regularity are in some cases more important for Crystal-Golden children than for Crystal children because if these three are not taken care of then the body shuts off to cooperation with the outside world. The body simply says "STOP!" when it cannot take any more because it is far more knowledgeable about what it needs than the parents or anyone else may be.

Negative imprinting will of course leave its mark on the Crystal and Crystal-Golden children of the future but as soon as they begin to have positive imprinting, it will not take long for their body cells to adapt to the new positive situation. Children are in fact quick to sense when the energy is positive and when it is negative and they will always gravitate towards the best, most balanced energy. Crystal-Golden children also give priority to being with joyful people who radiate life in their bodies.

Crystal children look before they leap, which Crystal-Golden children do not always think to do. They often jump straight into things, only to discover later that it would have been better to have been prepared. In general, though, there is no great behavioural difference between the two types of children, except that Crystal-Golden children are more body conscious and have more lust for life than Crystal children do.

The major difference between the two types of children is that Crystal-Golden children have the Golden energy activated at the cellular level in their bodies and that Crystal children do not, as yet. However, as soon as the time is right for them to be more outgoing and adventurous, the Golden energy will be activated.

∞ ∞ ∞ ∞ ∞ ∞ ∞ ∞ ∞

Crystal and Crystal-Golden adults of the future will be very aware of who they are and which human and professional skills they have. They will have clear opinions regarding many things and they will be fully conscious of their own position in life. They will not lie and will not like other people who lie. They will simply exclude such people from their lives without major explanations as to why. If people's life values do not match then there is no reason to try to get them to. So it is better to be with people where the balance is a natural state of affairs, without having to work at it.

They will be very conscious and consistent about what they accept and reject in life with regard to other people. They will know with whom they wish to have a close relationship and with whom they do *not* wish to be close in their daily lives and they will always lay their cards on the table in their relationships with other people.

Crystal youngsters, Crystal adults, and Crystal-Golden youngsters and adults will, in the future, be looking for the 'right' partner the very first time around. They will prefer not to make relationship 'mistakes' in the quest for the spirit mate whom they know exists. So they will prefer to wait a little longer for the right one to come along because they have no problem with keeping their own company. They will really want to have many exciting experiences while they are young but they will not want to make mistakes on the couple relationship front or with their studies.

Crystal and Crystal-Golden people cannot easily be made to doing something stupid just because other people are trying to make them. Balance and harmony in day-to-day life are important to them. They also like to feel super-comfortable in both of the places where they spend the most time - at home and at work. They need to feel a connection between their own basic philosophy of life and attitudes towards society and those of their employers, otherwise they will feel no loyalty to the latter. They should therefore be able to relate positively to the company's overall goals and visions, because otherwise their jobs will have no meaning for them.

Justice, balance and respect are important elements in all contexts in their lives, be it in their couple relationships, families, friendships, work, cooperations or the way they are paid. They are fully aware that they must, of course, contribute something extra to earn good money but they *cannot* be fooled and will not be bought off. They would rather walk away and start again elsewhere.

They need freedom with responsibility in all contexts but most clearly in their private lives and at work. It would also be most unlike them to behave purely selfishly. They also need to be able to see the ongoing development process of the projects with which they are involved, including their own personal development, because otherwise they lose their sparkle. Most importantly, they want to wield influence over the things that matter to them.

Their personal commitment will be much stronger than that of most adults with soul energy today, because they know that they have many life tasks in their body energy that are waiting to be released in order to be realised in their lives as soon as possible.

LOOK AFTER YOURSELF

Today, there are many spiritual people – including me – who take a lot of dietary supplements that are beneficial to us but when the Golden energy is activated in the Crystal body, it is important not to be tempted to take a lot of rejuvenating and revitalising health products, because they may not be appropriate for the energy structure in your body and in your consciousness. It is therefore important that you use your intuition to sense and then to choose what nutritional supplements best suit your current needs. Also, it may be a good idea to test your energy levels either with a naturopath, kinesiologist or similar practitioner or by using a frequency machine adapted for the New Time energy. However, many of the frequency machines that have been developed on the soul level are not adapted to people with Indigo, Crystal and Crystal-Golden energy.

High-frequency products and light healing may well be good for people with very condensed, heavy body energy who need to have their body frequency increased and there are many people like that on the soul level. However, if you have a very light energy structure, getting light healing or light contained in different kinds of dietary supplements can be like the equivalent of sending your body energy at high speed to Sirius or the Moon! If you do that, both you and all your body cells risk becoming ungrounded and if that happens, you will really need to focus on recreating balance in the body by choosing more balanced solutions.

It is also important to note that if you are always taking dietary supplements, your body will never get the chance to find out where it truly stands from a frequency point of view and whether it has moved too far away from your base frequency. So do take a break from nutritional supplements and body treatments from time to time, unless you know that you will get ill by stopping. By taking a break, you give your body the opportunity to show where it is when it is not having its energy either revved up or kept in check by health-promoting products or supplements.

The same applies to sugar, because the body would really like to have speed, sugar and light even though it does not need them. On the other hand, the brain does not want all that because it knows that it is not always good for the body to move up too high in frequency in relation to its basic frequency. This is because you risk becoming ungrounded and losing your personal balance by getting hyper and over-excited in exactly the same way that young children do when they have too much sugar.

The brain and the eyes cannot stand too much light – light in the form of energy and healing can actually be torture for both the brain and the eyes – because the brain in particular quickly loses its sense of time and space and the same goes for the eyes when they are dazzled by light, regardless of whether it comes from within your own energy system or from the outside.

Many body-crystallised people try, interestingly enough, to activate the Golden energy in their bodies by consuming a lot of dietary supplements, fruit (fruit sugar) and artificial sugar and this does help to increase cellular frequency, but dancing and taking part in a lot of sport works just as well and is even healthier. All physical activity actually helps to promote the activation of the Golden energy in the body. So you do not need help from a practitioner to activate the Golden energy in a Crystal body. All you need to do is to begin to live life and dare to do things that you maybe never dared to do before.

In other words, you are advised to jump at the deep end in your life and with both feet in order to truly feel it, provided of course that you have a Crystal body and want to activate the Golden energy at the cellular level. That is how the Crystal-Golden energy likes it. However, if you want to activate the Golden energy in your body energy but you are still on the soul level and therefore you are not yet body-crystallised, you are advised not to be over enthusiastic and start jumping into water that is too deep for you because you may well end up being selfish and smug. You may even completely stop using your head, because you lack the Crystal energy necessary to maintain your balance, to give you an overview, a feeling of responsibility and to help you keep your life in perspective.

Many people feel increased sexual desire when activating the Golden energy in the body – especially those on the soul level, as for them, the Golden energy goes directly into the lower abdomen – so it is very important for those people to maintain the balance in their own bodies if they do not want their libido to take over completely.

With a Crystal aura and body, you can also clearly feel that there is more activity in your life and your libido when the Golden energy is activated. Luckily, however, you will not end up in rehab for sex addiction! This is because the creative and inventive Golden impulse is often used to discover new ideas or to spark the entrepreneurial energy that people with Crystal-Golden energy have, almost around the clock rather than for the libido.

∞ ∞ ∞ ∞ ∞ ∞ ∞ ∞ ∞

In the current Crystal period, there are many hackers around in both the physical and the spiritual worlds. Common to them all is that they want access to your knowledge or your personal energy neither of which belong to them. Nevertheless, many try hard and it is not because they have Crystal energy in their auras, bodies and network energy that they try to access your energy. It is because you have Crystal energy integrated in these places and they hope and believe, quite wrongly, that by copying you, they will be led out onto the trail of their own life tasks and therefore become successful.

It is therefore important that you pay attention to always keeping a tight rein on your own energy, and that you remember to take your energy with you wherever you go, especially if you have Golden energy activated in your body, because other people can get really good mileage from their lives if they have access to your Golden 'fuel', vitality and joy of living.

However, if you have Crystal energy, they will do everything possible to 'photocopy' you because it is quite impossible to steal Crystal energy. However, others can copy you so much that you feel your personal and energy boundaries are being violated. They can even copy you to such an extent that, if you are not aware of it, you might even get sick because your energy system starts to burn at an exceptionally high rate to keep up with the energy copying, or because you are trying to burn the hacker's energy and physical attention away from your own energy system.

Energy copying of Crystal children can often cause fever at times when no one else is sick in the child's vicinity. So be aware that if your Crystal child suddenly develops a fever and it is not because the child has eaten something that disagrees with him/her, it may well be that adults with soul energy or youngsters with Indigo energy are in the process of copying your child's energy because they want the same pure energy and radiance for themselves.

As a human being with a Crystal aura and body, you should also be aware that there may be people on your path who think you are born under a star that is just a little too lucky. Consequently, they will send a lot of their own bad energies and negativity in your direction, so you have a little extra work and more challenges to deal with, which the people concerned think is very fair.

Unfortunately, most people do not understand that high-frequency consciousness, insight and balance is something that a large group of Crystal people have acquired through countless lives because of the experiences they have lived through, as well as through their own work-related and/or consciousness-related efforts. It is not just something they have earned by smiling sweetly at God before being sent to Earth this time around.

The people who send negativity and malicious thoughts and energies may well think that it serves you right to have some extra adversity in your life. So if you suddenly feel ill or you feel that bad energy is being sent in your direction, know that the bad energy cannot get into your body; it simply *cannot* when you have a Crystal aura. On the other hand, the negative energy can feel as intrusive as if there were a mass of paparazzi just outside your house, snapping away for dear life.

However, just because they are outside your home taking lots of pictures, it does not mean that they have access to your personal energy. All you have to do is to draw your curtains, close the shutters and pretend that nothing has happened, because then they will not be able to get any energy and attention from you and will soon slink off back to where they came from. That is also how it works with people who send bad energy in your direction. If you are not receptive to it, they will have to find another place to send it.

What you can also do in that situation, just as you would clean sticky finger marks off your windows, is to imagine that you are hosing your aura clean of other people's filth and that all the dirty water is going directly back to the people who have tried to cover you with their bad energy.

The best you can do, however, is to send back all the filth that they have thrown at your aura without even spending any time cleaning it. When you throw their energy straight back at them, all the signs that there have been demands on you and your energy will disappear. In this way, you have no further involvement in their negative and low-frequency energies. Their blueprint and energy footprint leave no trace on the outside of your aura. This means that no one else will get the same idea because, unfortunately, it is often the case that when one person succeeds in stepping over your boundaries, then several others will usually try to follow suit.

Always remember that if other people are staring at you and sending evil thoughts in your direction, they can get no energy from you if you have a Crystal aura and Crystal body. When you are crystallised in your aura and body, it is as if you need an angle grinder with a diamond cutter to get access to a even very small part of your energy.

It is only if you let yourself be convinced that they have gained access to your personal energy that you become weak and then they really can get access to your energy. They may not get direct access to your body energy but they can access your mental energy because you are thinking about, and therefore giving energy to, what has happened. In this way, you send your own pure Crystal energy back to them and this is exactly the energy that they really want to get hold of.

If you want to learn other ways to balance and take care of your own energy, then I highly recommend that you read the two easy-to-read energy guides written by my husband and me,

"The Little Energy Guide 1" and "Get Your Power Back Now!", and take our online course on energy sorting, which you can link to via **www.annisennov.com** and **www.fourelementprofile.eu**.

HOW TO SUCCEED IN YOUR OWN LIFE

When you want to succeed in life using the spiritual-materia-lising Golden energy in the Crystal body, it will be comforting for you to know that the Crystal energy supervises every aspect of your life. This is because the Crystal energy ensures, at all times, that your Golden energy meets its obligations regarding putting your dharma into practice. When things go wrong or fail to run completely smoothly, it will be impossible for you to stay in a bad mood and low in energy for very long. In the Crystal-Golden energy, there are always two opposing forces – the Crystal and Golden – to help you resurface, enabling you to quickly get on with life again.

When you want to succeed in your projects in the Crystal-Golden energy, you do not need to visualise the things you want to happen as you did on the soul level. It is better *not* to put words and images on your wishes at all but instead to let your body and all its cells know clearly that you want to succeed with certain things in the best possible way.

This does not mean that you cannot have any specific wishes in life; of course you can but maybe you will be even more success-ful if you are not locking yourself into things having to be done in a certain way. You can certainly wish for a holiday somewhere exotic but it is not certain that it will be the Maldives, which is what you might have been hoping for. However, maybe you will get an even more exotic experience by going to the Caribbean because there is a much better energy match between you and the Caribbean at the time of the trip than there is between you and the Maldives.

So let your Crystal-Golden body and the opportunities in the great wide world inspire you, because everything that happens around the world now on the human level is under the influence of the Crystal-Golden energy, even though the energies on the societal level remain under the influence of the Indigo and Crystal energies. It is not until around 2020 that the Crystal energy will start to emerge on the societal level around the world, when the young Crystals begin to find their way onto the job market.

Communicate with the Earth force just as much as you communicate with your own body, as it is from there that you will get all the help you need in the future in order to succeed. You have direct contact with God's power through your own body but your body is *not* God's power in all its glory. Your body is the messenger of divine energy, which is rendered visible through your actions in your daily life. So if you have an expanded con-sciousness and if your spiritual and material energies are pure, this will automatically be made visible to everyone, in the Crystal-Golden energy.

∞ ∞ ∞ ∞ ∞ ∞ ∞ ∞ ∞

It is actually contradictory to talk about succeeding with the help of the Crystal-Golden energy in the body, because in truth, you simply cannot fail when you have the Crystal-Golden energy integrated and activated in your body and your aura is Crystal. Your desires and your dharma will be one and the same, so you will not want to do things that are not in some way related to the implementation of your dharma. By focusing solely on succeeding with your life tasks, everything else will fall into place.

Consequently, I cannot come up with a lot of specific advice on how you can succeed in your life using the Crystal-Golden energy. Instead, I can encourage you to get your aura upgraded from the soul level to the spirit level – and therefore to the Crystal level – by having an AuraTransformation™ if you have not already had your aura transformed. In addition, I recommend that you focus 100% on putting your dharma into practice, as this is the main reason that you are alive on this planet right now, in this deeply transformative era on Planet Earth.

So if you are unsure of what your life task is, or what to do to succeed in a particular situation, think about what you would really love doing, because there is often a connection between your inner desires and your dharma and/or the solution to a current problem. Try to imagine yourself standing in the middle of your desired situation and feel whether it still seems exciting and right for you, because when you take the time to feel things properly in your body, it is often not as exciting and does not feel as right as you may originally have imagined.

If, for example, you want to be the spokesman/woman for a particular cause and you have problems expressing yourself in public it may not be such a good idea. Then you will need training in presentation skills and communication, as well as practice in speaking to many people at the same time. One solution to this might be that you go on a presentation skills course to get started on realising your innermost desires. It may well be however, that you change your mind along the way and decide to go in a different direction instead. However, the course will have helped you to make this decision and you will suddenly be one step closer to the implementation of your dharma, even if you still do not know what your dharma is.

Your body always knows what your dharma is and what the solution is to any given problem in your life but it does not comment directly on this. Instead, it lets you know when it feels really comfortable with different experiences and situations in life, so you get a clear hint that you are about to do something good for yourself and therefore often for other people too. Please listen to your amazing Crystal-Golden body and follow this impulse because then you simply cannot go wrong.

This also applies to trying things out, being open and taking risks in your daily life, as it is through your contact with other people that new doors will often open for you in the Crystal-Golden energy – doors that you may not even be able to see when you are seeking where it feels most natural for you to seek, but which other people may see every day because of their different energy frequencies. The social aspect is of far greater importance in the Crystal-Golden energy than in the Crystal energy, since nobody is actually able to find the way forward alone. All Crystal-Golden people have a continuous need for new input from the outside to feel really alive and inspired.

So once again, it is important to make a clear statement to your body and the Earth force about what you want. Life will then automatically guide you to the solution through your meeting new people with many different frequencies and element combinations on your way. Suddenly, the right job appears, along with your life partner and your new best friends, as well as the solutions to your current issues and problems. You just have to remember to open up to the opportunities that present themselves on your way and remember to keep sorting and cleaning the energy, so you do not get energy in your system which is not yours and which you therefore cannot use for something positive.

∞ ∞ ∞ ∞ ∞ ∞ ∞ ∞ ∞

As I said, it is still important to remember to sort energies so that you do not let yourself be influenced by other people's energies, negativity or what they may want for you. Always send other people's energies back to them in the form in which they were sent to you and pull your own rightful energy back from them and into your own body. Thus, you can be sure that you will not be influenced by their energies into taking a path that is not yours.

It is not only new influences you must remember to send back. Send back all the old influences from your past to other people too. If your body cells have been accustomed to such influences for many years and perhaps over a whole lifetime, begin to consciously communicate with your cells about what you would really like them to do instead of continuing with a particular negative behaviour or mind-set that has been brought about by these influences.

This is a conscious re-creation and transformation of your personal energy and balance on the love-intelligent level but I would recommend that you do not involve just anybody in the process, because those around you will often not be able to relate to your personal transformation. Keep it personal, because if those around you are primarily on the soul level, they will no longer have control over you when you begin succeeding with the re-creation and transformation of your personal energy and this will radically change the balance between you. Consequently, it is best if you keep these types of radical energy sorting projects to yourself until you feel that you feel solid enough and you feel that you are being set free from the influences of other people.

Indigos may also react with resistance when you start to set yourself free from past influences, even if the energy sorting does not involve them personally. This happens because on the inside, they feel overtaken by you without even having noticed that you were doing something differently... and also because they always want to know exactly what is going on! In fact, they prefer to take the initiative for change and transformation themselves, even when it comes to their immediate family and parents. They want to be the ones who make others aware that they need to change things in their lives!

People born with a lot of Golden energy on the soul level (because it is part of their karma and because they are part of a larger group on the survival level with extra Golden energy in their consciousness) will often create resistance when people with Crystal-Golden energy begin to clear out their past influences, because they lose their direct connection to the Crystal-Golden energy as a part of their platform. The Crystal-Golden people of the New Time have often taken on extra responsibility in family and/or social contexts, when they were still on the soul level in their auras and in their consciousness. As a result, there are many irresponsible people with lots of Golden energy in their families and close friends, etc., who now have to begin taking responsibility for their own lives and actions, which very few of them will want to do.

What separates a Crystal-Golden person from a soul-Golden person often becomes very clear and definitive when the Crystal-Golden person is finally rid of all the old influences, often to such an extent that the parties never really manage to be on the same wavelength again.

If the people you surround yourself with have almost no Golden energy in their bodies, they will often not be able to understand your creative inclinations in life and will react with either resistance or ignorance in relation to what you find most exciting and important.

If you are not yet body-crystallised, which means that the Golden energy cannot be activated in your body in a high-frequency balanced way, you can find yourself occasionally having resistance towards the Golden energy, quite simply because you are frustrated about not yet being able to feel a strong sense of joy in your life.

Even if you are in a well-functioning relationship, regardless of whether it is with your partner on a spirit or soul level, it is also important that you stay strong in your own energy and do not let yourself be influenced by what your partner wants you to be. The same applies to your children, other family members, friends and acquaintances. No one else must control your energy, even if they love you dearly.

It is always very good to be part of a positive and powerful community in the Crystal-Golden energy and since all communities consist of several individuals, it is extremely important that each individual feels and functions well and is in balance individually and not merely getting energy and attaining balance by being in the group. If just one person in the community is not feeling good, this will be reflected very clearly in the community's energy. The community would then be best served by dividing into two or more smaller groups, depending on how many members are parts of the Crystal-Golden community. These smaller groups each get the opportunity thereby to function optimally, while one or two people take care of the individuals who are not feeling good.

∞ ∞ ∞ ∞ ∞ ∞ ∞ ∞ ∞

Some people are born with more of the New Time Golden energy than others and this depends largely on their life tasks this time around. People with a predominance of New Time Golden energy often have many more and more diverse life tasks than people with a predominance of Crystal energy. On the other hand, the latter are often more dedicated and focused on performing selected tasks and projects in their lives, which they specialise in.

If you were born with a predominance of Golden energy in your body and it is the New Time powerful, holistic creative energy you have been carrying around in your body on the soul level, stuck inside your soul aura, there is no doubt that you will have appeared to be very provocative to those around you, especially your parents, countless times while you were growing up. This is because of your great ingenuity. You will also have been attracted by all sorts of exciting things that have popped up on your path that may have seemed totally meaningless to those around you. You have probably done some pretty strange things in your life and there will have been many ups and downs along the way, which have acted as two balancing opposites and dualities in your earthly life.

However, no one has such a life just for fun, or because it is premature for them from a consciousness perspective. All the life experience you may possibly have acquired through the many contradictory experiences you have had in your life up until now must be used in the Crystal-Golden energy, in a balanced way, to help others not to do the same. This is because most people listen with the greatest interest to those who have walked the path themselves; so the best counsellor and the greatest inspiration is the person who has done all the crazy things without reflecting on them, yet who has also experienced the lows that follow the wild times. By seeking your advice, other people in the Crystal-Golden energy will avoid paying the price of costly life lessons, enabling them to reach their goals more rapidly - goals that often have much more Crystal energy in them than Golden.

Through having had an extra amount of New Time Golden energy in the body at soul level while you were a child and teenager, you could, however, have subjected your body to a little too much instability, too many ups and downs in your life and too many ups and downs in your blood sugar. Bodily imbalances such as problems with kidneys, adrenal glands, thyroid and lower abdomen, as well as rheumatic fever and type 1 diabetes, could possibly occur in your life. You will therefore be forced to think much more than twice every time you decide to do something 'crazy'. You cannot just squander your own inner balance and bodily balance in that way. You will also be forced to think hard about how you live day by day, so that you do not find that your body suddenly hampers your creative efforts because you are pushing your body balance too hard.

For information purposes, type 2 diabetes belongs exclusively on the soul level, where people with a lot of Golden energy in their bodies have not been particularly aware of their own diet and lifestyle over the years. They will thus get a 'second chance' to catch up with changing their lives by being extra aware and responsible about their diet and lifestyle so they can slowly begin to crystallise in their bodies. Alternatively, many of them will begin to degenerate in their bodies, as there is not enough room for imbalances and irresponsibility on the body level in the Crystal-Golden energy.

∞ ∞ ∞ ∞ ∞ ∞ ∞ ∞ ∞

Some people deliberately choose to try to erase their old and uncomfortable physical memories, which is extremely foolish if they want to access some even deeper layers of their own body consciousness. This is because everything in the body is connected and you should therefore not delete experiences, knowledge or lessons learned from your consciousness, regardless of whether they are positive or negative. You must, on the contrary, raise them to a higher level of consciousness on the cellular level. You will then have the option of digging even deeper into your own cellular memory to acquire even more knowledge which will hopefully be positive, constructive and useful in your life, and perhaps it will even be possible here to get answers as to why you have previously experienced a lot of unpleasant things in your life, so the experiences end up making sense on the consciousness level.

If body memories are erased, the experiences will unfortunately have been of no use, which means that they will have to be repeated, in order for it to be possible for you to find your way further into the cellular memory to the next level of knowledge. Maybe those experiences are linked in one way or another to your karma at the soul level and/or your dharma on the spirit level. This would be like cutting off your nose to spite your face.

In terms of AuraTransformation™, all experience in the aura is lifted from the soul level to a much higher level of consciousness on the spirit level and the corresponding experience, which is stored as body memory in the cellular memory in the body, is lifted continuously to a higher level of consciousness due to body crystallisation. For those who have spontaneously lost their auras in connection with shocks, accidents and similar, all their previous life and consciousness experiences acquired at the soul level are united at a correspondingly higher level of consciousness in their auras when everything comes together on the Crystal level via an AuraTransformation™.

You can read more about this in my two books "The Crystal Human and the Crystallization Process Part I" and "Part II", which deal with everything you need to know about your body crystallisation process.

One thing you do need to know about the body crystallisation process, which most conscious people on Planet Earth are going to go through in order to lift their body consciousness to a higher level, is that you cannot just book a body treatment or balancing, and expect all your body crystallisation problems to be solved. This is because there is absolutely *no* short cut to body crystallisation - it is a consciousness-related process and a frequency shift which takes place in the most condensed part of your personal energy, namely in your body. Thanks to the body crystallisation process, you will get extraordinary insight into your own personal energy and the structure of your consciousness, as well as into where your own personal boundaries are. No one else can do this for you, no matter how clairvoyant they may be.

Most people hate their personal body crystallisation process with all their heart, which is very easy to understand. This is because as soon as the body is involved in any process, everything is felt with extra strong clarity and power, simply because the body is so condensed in its energy. It cannot therefore just ignore the problems, like the brain can but instead has to do something specific about them so that the body can quickly regain its balance on all levels.

Your inner child, which many spiritual people often focus on taking extra care of, is in fact your cellular memory on an emotional level, in which, of course, you must ensure balance in relation to your body crystallisation. Your body crystallisation therefore, is not only about the upgrading of the physical part of your body consciousness. Your body crystallisation is just as involved with upgrading your emotional and mental cellular memory, where the flow of energy is created at a higher level, instead of having blockages at a lower and not-so-intelligent consciousness level in the body.

When you are working to lift your body consciousness, you do not lose energy. Instead, you recycle the energy and knowledge that is released during the upgrading and transformation process in order to succeed at a higher level of consciousness. You will thus be able to remember all previous unpleasant experiences as an essential part of the knowledge in your body consciousness in order to prevent them from happening again, although you will not necessarily need to remember all the specific details.

If you have positive body memories from the past, then your body will simply upgrade the experiences to a higher level of consciousness, where they will be stored as essential knowledge in the body. You will then attract more positive experiences of the same kind, because they remind you of something good from the past.

I have personally met several high-frequency spiritual people who have had various unpleasant and bad experiences, lessons, feelings and thoughts removed and eliminated from their cellular memory, so they unfortunately cannot remember that they have had these experiences and why they have had them. It is almost like talking to someone with dementia who is beginning to let go of their terrestrial memory to slip quickly out of the terrestrial energy sphere. You can read about this in the chapter *The Moon* earlier in the book.

In fact, in my personal opinion, there is only one thing that the energy-related elimination method can be good at and that is to help people who have been subjected to torture and abuse to forget everything about the dreadful things they have been exposed to. This, however, presupposes that they have escaped far from where the torture is being carried out so as to not risk having to experience the same thing again; because if they cannot remember what they have experienced earlier, they will not be able to prevent it from happening again.

∞ ∞ ∞ ∞ ∞ ∞ ∞ ∞ ∞

If you want to succeed with the things in life that are important to you, it is best to bring your full pool of knowledge and experience with you everywhere and to lift your body frequency to a level where you feel comfortable and can think clearly. If the energy in your body is too low-frequency in relation to your personal basic energy, you will feel heavy in your body and if the energy in your body is too high, you will feel extra light and find it difficult to focus on succeeding at anything. Body balance really is the be all and end all for your success in all things.

When you have a fine Crystal balance in your body, and the Golden energy is activated at the cellular level, your personal qualities and strengths will naturally begin to find their way to the surface. Then, you can slowly begin to put them into practice where they will become visible to everyone else. So if, for example, you have extraordinary personal skills and strengths, these can no longer be held back in the body, unless their activation depends on very specific circumstances, in which case, the qualities in question are maybe predestined to be released at a later time when you can make much better use of them than you can right now.

EARTH AND ITS FUTURE

On my intensive, consciousness-developing planet courses which I regularly run in different countries, I am frequently asked: "What will happen to the Earth when we begin to integrate the different energies from the planets around the solar system?"

The answer is very simple because what will happen is exactly what has already happened on Earth. The planetary energies of our own solar system have, for the most part, been here all along, in various combinations. The planetary energies exist in everyone all over Planet Earth and many people even have energy within them that originates from planets, solar systems and galaxies outside of our own solar system.

All the energies are already here and many of them have been here for hundreds of thousands of years. Consequently, integrating new external energies is not the solution to the overall integration problems in our solar system. Rather, it is important to get rid of all the energies that do not operate in a balanced way together with the other planetary energies here on Earth. If they are not working on Planet Earth, they will not work in a balanced way out in the solar system either and they will never be able to adapt to their surroundings. They must therefore be eliminated forever in a terrestrial framework in order also to be eliminated from the solar system and further out in the Cosmos.

There is not a single aspect of the various planetary energies present here on Earth that has not had an honest and fair chance to show who they are and what they can contribute to the Whole. If they cannot contribute something positive on Earth, they cannot contribute something positive to the Cosmos either, as all the other energies in the Cosmos and in Earth's interior Golden energy, which represents creation and the creative power in the Cosmos, have been finely tuned in relation to each other.

In the Crystal-Golden Age, we will therefore experience the elimination of many different types of energies and characteristics that will not be acceptable anywhere in the world, regardless of where they have originated on Planet Earth or in the solar system. There are therefore certain planetary frequencies and vibrations that will be eliminated from the energy sphere of Earth and the solar system, never to return.

Among the frequencies which will be eliminated in the future are violence and aggression, mistreatment of others, whether people or animals, malice towards and discrimination against people who are different from you as well as smoking and drug abuse along with many other unfortunate characteristics and trends. These characteristics and trends will all disappear as the people who have those characteristics and needs begin to disappear from the face of Planet Earth; in other words, when they die.

Should these people want to come back to Earth later, this will not be possible unless they have eliminated and upgraded the unfortunate personal characteristics and needs to some higher vibrational characteristics and needs before they are born. So here, we really can talk about eliminating energies and knowledge forever if individuals do not have anything positive to contribute to the Whole. However, most individuals who do not have something good in them will not get the opportunity to return to Earth in their original energy forms. They will then be forced to merge with their opposite from a consciousness perspective and their dual on the spirit level in order to expand 'the duo's' common consciousness capacity.

This means that next time around they will be born with a

greater consciousness consisting of two former conscious-nesses in one and the same body that would be adapted to the actual conditions on Earth at that point in time. However, the inappropriate consciousnesses may be forced to merge with both their own dual and additionally with one or more other dual couples, each consisting of two duals, in order to be able to sufficiently raise frequency to fit into energy level of the Earth at the time when they are reborn here on the planet.

Alternatively, those consciousnesses that do not have anything positive to contribute to the Whole here on Earth, will be return-ed to their planet of origin to be upgraded there, using the ways and means of that planet.

One of the reasons that new energies will not be constantly coming into the terrestrial energy sphere during the next hun-dred years is that it is now time for us to balance the existing energies on Earth. In addition, all the planets in the solar system will jointly filter off the best and strongest energies from each of the different planets and this will then be transferred to all future new-born children here on Planet Earth.

The best and strongest energies will not be explained from the perspective of planet energy but rather, from the perspective of the energy of the elements. Therefore, no child today who has Crystal or Crystal-Golden energy will ever need to focus on integrating the selected planetary characteristics in their consciousness. On the other hand, they will have to strengthen the qualities of the four elements in their personal energy and behaviour on both the Crystal level and the Golden level in their bodies, since they already have the four elements integrated in their personal consciousness from birth. However, they can always usefully reinforce these elements so that they can expand the scope of their consciousness in different areas of life.

It is therefore no longer necessary for adults to integrate the characteristics of the planets in our solar system, whether they are on soul level or spirit level with their consciousness. This is because it is much easier and more manageable to focus on integrating the four elements in their personal energy and behaviour, instead of a lot of different planetary energies whose data is forever changing.

∞ ∞ ∞ ∞ ∞ ∞ ∞ ∞ ∞

Earth is a living organism, just like the human body. As a result, all life that exists in Earth's interior will be mirrored both in the human body and in people's mental, emotional and spiritual consciousness. When Earth raises its consciousness frequency, which will happen as it opens up for more of its own energy in Earth's interior and more Golden energy is released, then the human body will correspondingly need to open up more to its inherent consciousness.

This will be expressed in the future in many different ways. People on the planet will be more creative, innovative and responsible. Sex will still be an interesting phenomenon in the terrestrial sphere, since it is an optimal way to exchange energy right down into the deepest levels of the consciousness of the parties involved. There will, however, be a tendency in the future, to not exchange energy in this intimate way with just any old person to whom you may feel physically and humanly attracted. Most people will be attracted to their spirit mates, that is to say the person with whom they are destined to merge on the spirit level at a specific time in the couple's joint consciousness development.

In the future, we will see that young people do not have many love affairs before they get married with their one and only, and we will experience broad-mindedness and freedom in the couple relationship where both parties are allowed to party and have fun with other people. We will also experience that homosexuals everywhere on Earth will be allowed to marry each other if they love each other. Economically based relationships – regardless of whether they occur between heterosexuals or homosexuals – will very soon be things of the past, because Crystal-Golden young people will never take those who can be bought or who are only attracted by money seriously, nor will they respect them.

Everyone with Crystal-Golden energy and a Crystal aura will be able to feel their own Golden life force in their bodies and will also be very aware of their own responsibility in relation to lifting the energy level around the world in their own particular ways. The Golden energy is not an extraordinary power needing extra focus or struggle in order to connect with it in their bodies. It is just there because it is their vitality, their creation and creative power, without which they cannot live.

Crystal-Golden people use the Golden energy to keep themselves happy and vibrant in everyday life; they use it for sex, for celebrating and for inspiring other people at work and at play. They also use it to put their dharma into practice. The Golden energy is as versatile as any Crystal-Golden person decides that it can be.

∞ ∞ ∞ ∞ ∞ ∞ ∞ ∞ ∞

In the future, alternative medicine and traditional medicine will work together here on Earth, since chemically produced medicine will only be necessary when there are no naturally produced products and methods to promote the body's own healing power. Furthermore, the pharmaceutical industry will increasingly begin to make use of stem cell cultivation in connection with the healing of serious physical illnesses and chronic suffering.

Surgery will still be carried out on the human body, according to each person's bodily and personal needs. However, we will see that people will be more easily satisfied with their looks, as the Golden energy is predominantly very happy with its own appearance. People with Golden energy will therefore see no immediate reason to change their appearance. They will try instead to highlight the physical benefits that they have, instead of removing what they are not happy with. So here the Crystal energy with its strong focus on being perfect will have to make some compromises on its inner beauty ideals!

The use of Botox for lips and skin, along with many other similar inventions, will begin to show their most unpleasant sides, where people who want to be beautiful will instead look like monsters because poison has been injected into their faces and bodies. In addition, many people who take steroids in large quantities may find that their muscles will wither, because there is no balanced Crystal-Golden energy in either their muscles or in the rest of their body energy. This is because steroids do not contribute to body crystallisation in a balanced way. Instead, they distort the cell structure of the muscles.

The human body of the future will *not* respond positively to the use of unbalanced products and medication, unless the products and medicines are necessary for the person to survive. In this case, the Crystal-Golden body will be very aware that this is the case and it will try to adapt itself as best as it can to the intake of such products or medicines. However, it will be necessary to try to balance and strengthen the body to an exceptional extent in other areas so that it is not exposed to a constant, far too one-sided influence and stress from such products and medicines.

The concepts of Light and Darkness will start to be on as equal a level as the main energies here on Earth, so there will no longer be a tendency to dichotomise them and describe them as being either positive or negative. Instead, the main focus will be on balancing the two energies in everyone and in everything that exists on Planet Earth.

Light will thus help your mind to feel at ease and in touch with your spirit energy, while Darkness will help your body to have a more solid structure, helping you to be more visible in relation to those around you – and Light is actually not of a higher frequency than Darkness.

Today there are many people around the world who have a high-frequency condensed energy structure and therefore Darkness in their energy systems who are helping the world to balance and develop on the physical level. If there were only Light energy on the planet, Earth and all human and animal bodies would slowly disappear, as would our materialisation power. Light is really pure energy and radiance, which means that we cannot always feel our physical problems and limitations so clearly, meaning that healing with pure Light rarely helps to solve physical problems and bodily disabilities.

Darkness is not identical with negativity and evil, as many spiritual people mistakenly believe, so do not spend time fighting Darkness, which is simply condensed light and energy. It is the evil in people and their negative intentions which you need to combat.

∞ ∞ ∞ ∞ ∞ ∞ ∞ ∞ ∞

Another thing that it is appropriate to fight here on Earth is ignorance and great efforts will be made here in the Crystal-

Golden Age. This is because the Crystal-Golden energy knows that it is totally impossible to lift the knowledge and frequency levels around the world if people are kept ignorant about life and general human conditions and about which development opportunities and ways of life exist in other cultures and other places around the world.

The level of knowledge will generally be increased on the community level everywhere on Earth, even in the more established and well-functioning societies where the existing framework of society is often used to control people and keep them within that framework rather than to help them to realise their own potential. However, it is important to maintain balance. This means that in the future, help and support will not be given to people without them giving equivalent help to other people, unless they are obviously incapable of doing this.

The Crystal-Golden energy is a strong advocate of the 'be helped and then help others' principle, where the person who has been helped by others, or by society and the state, tries at all times to help other people to have a better life and to function better, so that they can, in turn, help others to have better lives. In this way, a positive energy spiral will quickly spread over the Earth matrix like ripples in water.

Today, there are many different forms of common consciousness, collective consciousness and group consciousness around the world, which the people of Earth will have to decide whether to be a part of or not. Even if you are born in a specific country and into a specific family line, it is not certain that you will feel in tune with the energy of the country of your birth or with the energy of your family. It is therefore important for you to leave the established group consciousnesses behind and instead get together with people in other groups where you feel comfortable.

This will happen to a much greater extent than before all over the world, where no one in the future will falsely or reluctantly hand over energy to communities of which they are no longer a part or that they cannot vouch for.

This will be true for example for former colleagues, as well for people who, because of a single common denominator, such as the same type of job, leisure interest or physical disorder, are part of a specific group where others can consciously or unconsciously feed on their energy. This will also apply to former alcoholics, drug addicts and others who have beaten their addiction, where they will have to release the state of consciousness that led to the addiction in order to be able to move forward in their lives.

So when people in the future leave a certain group or community, those they leave behind will often feel that they are no longer part of the community and when they choose to join a new community, the common energy will change noticeably wherever they join.

∞ ∞ ∞ ∞ ∞ ∞ ∞ ∞ ∞

If you want to activate the Golden energy into your Crystal body by travelling around the world, I will conclude by sharing some travel suggestions with you, because the Golden energy in its purest form has an exceptionally strong presence in South Africa, Australia, Norway, in some parts of Japan as well as in selected states in the USA, where there are direct openings to the Golden energy of Earth on the energy level. So you could benefit from travelling to these countries and areas to increase your materialisation power even more. However, do not forget that it is important that you have the Crystal energy fully integrated in every cell in your body, because if you just integrate the Golden energy without first having the Crystal energy in place, you are not going to succeed with your future projects.

It could also be an advantage to have the Venus-Crystal energy integrated into your body in the three Scandinavian countries - Norway, Sweden and Denmark - where AuraTransformation™ is very widespread. This is because the Crystal energy is present everywhere in the social structures in those countries and the energy spreads out from there, into the world.

You can also have the Crystal energy in your aura integrated in many countries around the world, mainly in Europe, by having an AuraTransformation™. You can read more about this on **www.auratransformation.com**.

If you want to experience a combination of very structurally complete and visionary Crystal energy and the productive and very creative and internationally focused Golden energy, I would definitely recommend that you visit Dubai. This is truly a Crystal-Golden metropolis and it was there that I finished writing this book. I really felt the Crystal-Golden energy both outside on the community level as well as in my own energy system. The last three chapters of the book were written in Dubai and the first proofreadings, by myself and my dear husband, also took place in Dubai.

THANK YOU FOR READING

As you may already have sensed from reading this book, I have extensive knowledge about the Indigo and Crystal energies, the Crystal-Golden and the Golden energies, as well as many other forms of energy in our solar system and around the Cosmos. In addition, I constantly get new, exciting ideas and am continuously implementing new projects in the hope of helping other people to become more conscious of their own energy and also to feel better. This, in turn, enables them to help even more people to make a positive difference here on Planet Earth, both for themselves and for others.

At first, the Crystal energy was my favourite energy, and then the Golden energy became my favourite energy and as I write this book, the Crystal-Golden energy is my favourite. I have felt at home in all three energies and I will certainly do so in the Diamond energy too, if I am still alive when it becomes visible on Earth's surface.

I love life, although I did not always, as I have had many challenges both in my life and in my body. I therefore try hard to get others to love their lives too, so that they can begin to live their dharma, just as I am living my dharma. I do this partly by running the spiritual Elements and Planet courses, workshops with a focus on element activation in the body, as well as activation of the Golden energy in the body, etc. In addition, I run group-based online transformational webinars for aura-transformed people in different countries who want help getting in touch with their own dharma and want to network with other like-minded spiritually oriented people.

I have also written many books about the New Time energy and consciousness, and most importantly of all, I work every day with my husband and spirit mate Carsten Sennov who conti-nually supports and encourages me to bring my own projects and our many joint new projects and initiatives to fruition.

You can read more about my many different activities on **www.annisennov.com**, where you can also read articles, watch videos and look at my calendar, as well as sign up for my Danish and English newsletters. You can also register on my English blog – it is free to become a member.

If you have not already read my previous books, some of which have been translated into different languages, then I warmly recommend that you do this. The books deal with various themes that are very relevant to the New Time energy. To give you a quick overview of the content of some of the books, please read the list below:

"Balance on All Levels with the Crystal and Indigo Energies"

- Insight into the energies of Indigo and Crystal children, as well as 'transitional' children
- Facts about AuraTransformation™ and the new aura structures
- Personal and general changes associated with an AuraTransformation™
- The first five dimensions of the consciousness of Earth
- The difference between spirit and matter
- Conscious use of energy and the magic in everyday life
- The masculine and feminine energies

"The Crystal Human and the Crystallization Process Part I" and "Part II"

- The Crystal energy
- The overall development from soul to Crystal energy
- The 13 dimensions of consciousness in the Earth's energy
- Introduction to the four elements
- Detailed information on the body crystallisation process and lots of case studies
- Information about the children and adolescents of the New Time and their consciousness

"Spirit Mates – The New Time Relationship"

- The three types of couple relationship on Earth
- Connectedness in the spirit
- The common life task

"Karma-free in the New Time"

- What does it mean to be karma-free?
- Earth's spiritual energy structure
- The structure of the Shamballah force

"The Little Energy Guide 1"

- Energy sorting exercises for all

"Get Your Power Back Now!"

This is the book that all parents will wish they had had the opportunity to read when they were children!!!

- Effective introduction to the use of energy for children and young people in everyday life as well as for their parents
- Lots of efficient energy methods and energy sorting exercises

"Be a Conscious Leader in Your Own Life" *(in Danish and Swedish only)*

- How to change your personal energy, behaviour and priorities
- Communicate with your inner voice
- The four element profile™ personality type model
- Description of the four elements and all element combinations
- Capture your full potential
- Find the red thread in your life

You will find a list of all the current books written by my husband and me in different languages on **www.annisennov.com**.

Thank you for reading ☺

With love,

Anni Sennov
December 2014

ABOUT ANNI SENNOV

Anni Sennov is the founder of **AuraTransformation™** and of **the Aura Mediator Courses™** which take place in different countries mainly in Europe.

She is a clairvoyant advisor, international lecturer and the author of more than 20 books about energy, consciousness and self-development, as well as New Time children and relationships, several of which have been translated from Danish into a number of languages.

Together with her husband Carsten Sennov, she is a partner in the publishing company Good Adventures Publishing and the management consulting and coaching company SennovPartners, where she is a consultant in the fields of personal development, energy and consciousness.

Anni and Carsten Sennov have developed the personality type indicator **four element profile™** that consists of four main energies corresponding to the four elements of Fire, Water, Earth and Air, which are each present in everyone in a variety of combinations of balance and strength.

Multiple courses are offered on how to understand and integrate these elements both for private people as well as businesses.

Anni Sennov was born in Denmark in 1962 and originally began her career in the financial world. Since 1993 she has had her own practice of personal counselling and her great strength is her ability to clairvoyantly perceive multiple relevant circumstances pertaining to her clients' personality and consciousness.

Anni Sennov's work and books are mentioned in numerous

magazines, newspapers and on radio and television in many countries.

You can connect to Anni Sennov's profile on Linkedin, Google+, Twitter and Facebook, where she has an English author profile:

facebook.com/pages/Anni-Sennov/141606735859411

You can subscribe to her English newsletter, become a member of her blog and see her travel schedule and event calendar at **www.annisennov.com**.

THE SOUL AURA

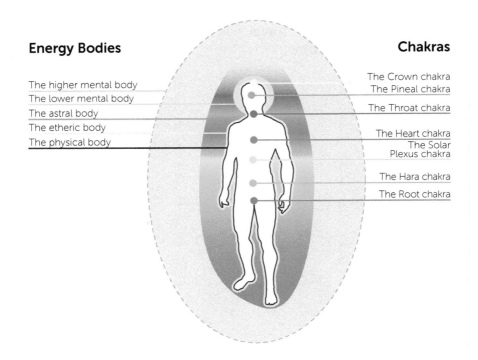

Energy Bodies

The higher mental body
The lower mental body
The astral body
The etheric body
The physical body

Chakras

The Crown chakra
The Pineal chakra
The Throat chakra
The Heart chakra
The Solar Plexus chakra
The Hara chakra
The Root chakra

THE INDIGO AURA

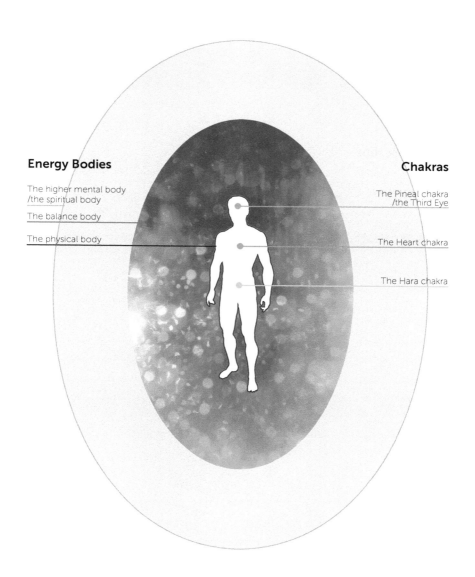

Energy Bodies

The higher mental body
/the spiritual body

The balance body

The physical body

Chakras

The Pineal chakra
/the Third Eye

The Heart chakra

The Hara chakra

THE CRYSTAL AURA

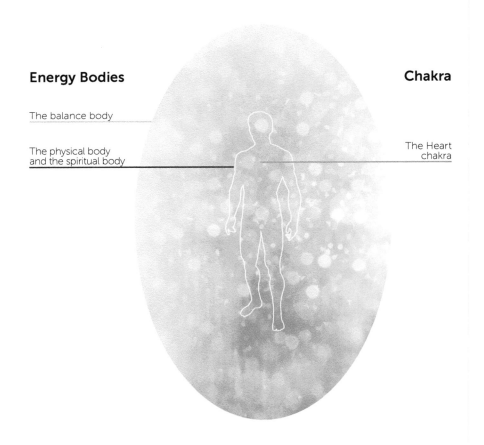

Energy Bodies

The balance body

The physical body
and the spiritual body

Chakra

The Heart
chakra

THE CRYSTAL-GOLDEN AURA

Energy Bodies

Chakra

The balance body

The physical body
and the spiritual body

The Heart
chakra

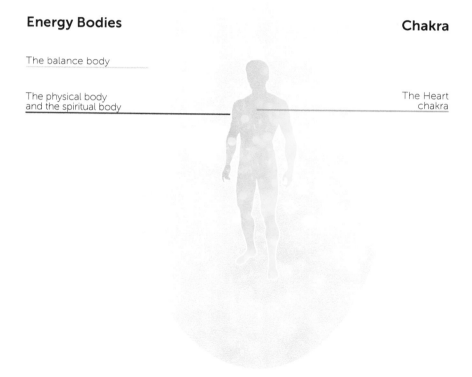